WRITING EXPOSITORY PARAGRAPHS

With Enabling Writing Activities and Grammar Exercises

Second Edition
Revised Printing

Hayib N. Sosseh

Northern Virginia Community College

Kendall Hunt
publishing company

Cover image © Shutterstock, Inc.

Kendall Hunt
publishing company

www.kendallhunt.com
Send all inquiries to:
4050 Westmark Drive
Dubuque, IA 52004-1840

Copyright © 2004, 2010 by Kendall Hunt Publishing Company
Revised Printing 2013

ISBN 978-1-4652-2062-2

Printed in the United States of America
10 9 8 7 6 5 4 3

CONTENTS

Acknowledgments. vii

To the Teacher viii

To the Student. ix

INTRODUCTORY UNIT

The Paragraph 1

Objectives 1
Paragraph Format 2
Generating Ideas 2
The Topic Sentence 3
Support Sentences 4
Unity 4
Coherence 5
The Concluding Sentence 6
The Complete Sentence 8
  Phrases and Clauses 9
  Non-Idiomatic or Awkward Sentences . . . 13
Enabling Grammar Exercises 15
Subjects 15
  Subject Pronouns 15
Linking Verbs and Action Verbs 17
  Linking Verbs 17
  Action Verbs 18
Transitive and Intransitive Verbs 19
Subject–Verb Agreement 20
Editing. 22
Paragraph Analysis 23

UNIT ONE

Example. 25

Objectives 25
Part I: The Example Paragraph 25
Paragraph Analysis 26
**Part II: Elements of an Example
  Paragraph** 27
The Topic Sentence of an Example
  Paragraph 27

Support Sentences. 29
Detailing Support Sentences 30
The Concluding Sentence 32
**Part III: Writing Your Example
  Paragraph** 34
Expressing an Opinion about a Topic 34
Generating Ideas to Support an Opinion 35
Prioritizing Ideas 36
Writing a Rough Draft 39
Part IV: Enabling Grammar Exercises. . . . 40
Structure and Use of the Simple Present
  Tense 40
Basic Sentence Structure—Simple
  Present Tense 40
Use of Simple Present Tense 40
Opinions 41
Factual Statements 42
Habitual Activities 43
Use of Frequency Adverbs 43
Personal Information about Self or Others. . . 45
Determiners. 46
Articles 46
Quantifiers. 48

UNIT TWO

Process 53

Objectives 53
Part I: The Process Paragraph 53
Paragraph Analysis 54
Part II: Elements of a Process Paragraph . 55
The Topic Sentence of a Process Paragraph. . 55
Support Sentences. 57
The Concluding Sentence 59
Part III: Writing Your Process Paragraph. 61
Differentiating Between Chronologically
  Ordered and Spatially Ordered
  Paragraphs. 61
Getting Ideas for Chronologically Ordered
  Paragraphs. 64
Categorizing Steps in a Process 65

Getting Ideas for Spatially Ordered
Paragraphs. 66
Categorizing Pierced Parts by Location 67
Part IV: Enabling Grammar Exercises. . . 69
Prepositions. 69
Ordinals. 72

UNIT THREE

Description 75

Objectives 75
Part I: The Descriptive Paragraph 75
Paragraph Analysis 76
**Part II: Elements of a Descriptive
Paragraph** 77
The Topic Sentence of a Descriptive
Paragraph 77
Support Sentences. 79
The Concluding Sentence 80
**Part III: Writing Your Descriptive
Paragraph** 81
Generating Ideas 81
Describing a Person 82
Describing an Object 84
Describing a Scenery or View 85
Sensory Details 87
Part IV: Enabling Grammar Exercises. . . . 92
Action / Non-action Verbs 92
Noun Clauses 94

UNIT FOUR

Narration 99

Objectives 99
Part I: The Narrative Paragraph 99
Paragraph Analysis 100
**Part II: Elements of a Narrative
Paragraph** 101
The Topic Sentence. 101
The Support of a Narrative Paragraph 102
The Concluding Sentence 103
Proverbs and Sayings as Lessons or
Morals. 104
**Part III: Writing Your Narrative
Paragraph** 104
Getting Ideas. 104
Writing a Rough Draft 105
Editing. 105

Part IV: Enabling Grammar Exercises. . . 106
Direct Speech and Reported Speech. 106
Statement. 108
Information Question 108
Yes/No Question 108
Command 108
Command with the Negative
Marker "Not" 109

UNIT FIVE

Extended Definition 111

Objectives 111
Part I: Extended Definition 111
Paragraph Analysis 112
**Part II: Elements of an Extended
Definition** 113
Single Sentence Definition as Topic
Sentence 113
Definition Sentence. 113
Hyphenated Noun Phrase 114
Adjectives 116
Distinguishing Characteristics as Adjective
Clauses 118
**Part III: Writing Your Extended
Definition** 120
Generating Ideas 120
Determining Class of Subject 120
Listing Distinguishing Characteristics 122
Constructing One-sentence Definition 124
Outline for the Extended Definition
Paragraph 125
Circular Definition 127
Writing a Rough Draft 128
Part IV: Enabling Grammar Exercises. . . 129
Adjectives Clauses 129
Using Adjective Clauses to Identify
a Person. 130

UNIT SIX

Cause and Effect 135

Objectives 135
**Part I: The Cause and Effect
Paragraph** 135
Paragraph Analysis 136
**Part II: Elements of a Cause and Effect
Paragraph** 136

The Topic Sentence of a Cause and Effect
    Paragraph 136
Support Sentences of a Cause and Effect
    Paragraph 137
The Concluding Sentence 139
Part III: Writing Your Cause and Effect
    Paragraph 140
Generating Ideas 140
Determining Causes of Accidents 141
More Anecdotes 141
Possible Causes of Accidents 144
Analysis of Cause Effect Sentences 145
Punctuating Cause Effect Sentences 147
Cause Effect Statements 149
Modal Auxiliaries in Cause Effect
    Sentences 150
Part IV: Enabling Grammar Exercises . . . 151
Modals 151
Modals and Their Meanings 151
Negative Modals 152
Modals in the Past Tense 153
Other Uses of Modals 155

UNIT SEVEN

Comparison and Contrast . . . 157

Objectives 157
Part I: The Comparison and Contrast
    Paragraph 157
Types of Comparison and Contrast
    Paragraphs 158
Paragraph Analysis 159
Part II: Elements of a Comparison
    and Contrast Paragraph 160
The Topic Sentence 160
Comparison and Contrast Support
    Sentences 162
The Concluding Sentence 165
Part III: Writing Your Comparison
    and Contrast Paragraph 166
Generating Ideas 166
Deciding What to Compare or Contrast 169
Deciding Whether to Compare or
    Contrast 171
Listing Similarities and Differences 173
Part IV: Enabling Grammar Exercises . . . 176
Coordinators 176
Conjunctive Adverb or Adverb Phrase 180
Correlative Conjunctions 181

UNIT EIGHT

Classification 185

Objectives 185
Part I: The Classification Paragraph 185
Paragraph Analysis 186
Part II: Elements of a Classification
    Paragraph 187
The Topic Sentence of a Classification
    Paragraph 187
Writing a Topic Sentence 188
Developing a Classification Paragraph 189
Ordering of Categories 191
The Concluding Sentence 192
Restating a Topic Sentence 192
Part III: Writing Your Classification
    Paragraph 195
Generating Ideas 195
Determining Principles for Classification . . . 196
Writing Classification Sentences 198
Punctuating Classification Sentences 200
Classification Sentences in the Active
    Voice or Passive Voice 200
Part IV: Enabling Grammar
    Exercises 203
Passive Voice and Active Voice 203
The "By Phrase" 207
Participial Adjectives 208

UNIT NINE

Argumentation 211

Objectives 211
Part I: The Argumentative Paragraph . . . 211
Paragraph Analysis 212
Part II: Elements of an Argumentative
    Paragraph 214
Stating the Issue 214
Taking a Stand 217
Analyzing Sentences That Express
    a Stance 219
Giving Reasons for and Against
    Your Stance 222
Supporting Ideas 224
Refutation 225
Part III: Writing Your Argumentative
    Paragraph 227
Generating Ideas 227
Controversial Issues 227

Vocabulary Used in Argumentation 229
Part IV: Enabling Grammar Exercises. . . 231
Adverb Clauses. 231
Sentence Types 234

UNIT TEN

Introduction to the Essay . . . 239

Objectives 239
**Part I: Paragraphs and Essays:
    Similarities and Differences**. 239
Part II: The Essay. 240
Essay Analysis 241
Part III: Elements of the Essay 243
Attention Grabber 243
Thesis Statement. 243
Body Paragraphs. 244
Relevance of Support Sentences in Body
    Paragraphs. 247
Concluding Paragraph. 248

Part IV: Writing Your Essay 248
Generating Ideas 248
Categorizing Ideas 249
Forming Sentences with Words or
    Phrases in Categories 250
Writing a Draft 251
Editing. 252
Part V: Enabling Grammar Exercises . . . 253
Causative. 253
*Type A: Causative Verbs That Take
the Base Form of the Verb in the
Second Clause* 253
*Type B: Causative Verbs That Take
the Infinitive in the Second Clause* 256

Index 261

ACKNOWLEDGMENTS

I wish to thank Charlotte Calobrisi, a colleague, for her invaluable support. Her insights, suggestions, and willingness to read rough drafts and units were instrumental in the writing of this text. My sincere thanks to Susan Hollins and Leslie Czaplicki for helping me solve computer-related problems that came up more often than I expected.

I am grateful to my ESL colleagues at Northern Virginia Community College (NVCC) for their support and encouragement. I wish to acknowledge the faculty and staff in the Languages and Literature Division, Annandale Campus for their support and Dr. Robert Templin, Jr. President, Northern Virginia Community College for his permission to use the list of steps in the process for getting started at NVCC.

I also wish to acknowledge Shahnaz Masumi, Quang Trinh, Sana Hilmi, Kumju Park, Shirley Lee, Abdulmonam Alikaj, Weiwei Wang, and Lianfang Shu for their help, as native speakers of their respective languages in translating certain words, sentences, and concepts into English.

I am indebted to my students, who have taught me so much about their languages and cultures. My special thanks to those students whose work we have included in the text.

I wish to thank Curtis Ross, Billee Jo Hefel, Angela Puls and Jessica Cannavo of Kendall Hunt Publishing for their professionalism and interest in how the project was progressing during the development and production stages.

TO THE TEACHER

This text is designed to make the tasks of generating ideas and writing paragraphs less daunting. The focus of the text is paragraph format and the necessary elements of sentences and paragraphs of various rhetorical styles. For each type of paragraph development, there are tasks that enable students to go through the writing process while learning rhetoric-specific format, sentence structures, and punctuation.

The introductory unit helps students become familiar with paragraph organization, topic sentences, support sentences, and concluding sentences. Also covered are structure and importance of the complete sentence in written language, paragraph unity, and coherence.

Units one through nine cover nine different modes of paragraph development. Each of these units has activities that enable students to express their opinions, share ideas, and learn vocabulary and mechanics they may need to write a paragraph using a particular rhetorical mode. In addition, each unit has enabling grammar exercises that provide students with more practice on the grammar patterns used in writing a paragraph in the rhetorical style discussed in the unit. In unit ten, students are introduced to the essay format and the elements of an essay.

TO THE STUDENT

A paragraph is an important unit of written text. In it, a writer introduces and develops one idea. As you write a paragraph in English, you need to know what an English paragraph looks like, its elements, and different methods of development.

This text is designed to help you write different kinds of paragraphs. To begin with, you will be asked to participate in activities to generate ideas. These situations will make it possible for you to express your ideas orally and to exchange points of view with your classmates. During these participatory activities, you will learn and use language, vocabulary, and other devices you will need to compose and edit different types of paragraphs.

Units one through nine are designed to help you learn how to write paragraphs in which you use certain forms of argument and ordering of ideas. Unit ten introduces you to the format and elements of an essay, the next level in the writing process. You will also learn the process of writing an essay. The text includes activities and tasks that are designed to help you deal with problems that often appear in intermediate-student writing.

In each of units one through nine, you will learn the types of sentences the paragraph is made of: topic sentence, support sentences, and concluding sentence. These types of sentences may vary depending on the type of expository paragraph being written. You will systematically learn to recognize, analyze, create, and use such sentences as you write different types of paragraphs. Also included in each unit are exercises that are designed to help you with grammatical structures you may need to write the paragraph in question.

INTRODUCTORY UNIT
The Paragraph

OBJECTIVES

By the end of this unit, you should be able:

- ■ to state the distinctive features of a paragraph
- ■ to identify the topic sentence, support sentences, and concluding sentence of a paragraph
- ■ to define paragraph unity and coherence
- ■ to recognize a complete, well-formed sentence

A paragraph is a group of sentences that develop one main idea (topic). There are three types of sentences within the paragraph: the topic sentence, support sentences, and the concluding sentence. Generally, the topic sentence, which is the main idea, is the first sentence; however, some paragraphs have the topic sentence in the middle, others have it at the end and in still other paragraphs, the topic sentence is implied. Nonetheless, putting the topic sentence at the beginning will help you to organize your paragraph.

The support sentences, which generally follow the topic sentence, help to develop the main idea of the paragraph. The types of supporting ideas used in a paragraph depend on the method of development. Support sentences may be descriptions, statements of fact or opinion, or sentences that provide detail.

Concluding sentences vary depending on the type of paragraph. A common type of concluding sentence is a restatement of the topic sentence. Another type is a summary sentence. A concluding sentence can also be a statement that gives the result of a process, reiterates the main idea, or one that looks to the future. Although a paragraph can be as long as you think is necessary to develop the main idea, expository paragraphs are generally between 7 and 15 sentences long.

Paragraph Format

Paragraphs should follow a certain format. To begin with, the first line of a paragraph is indented. The indentation is what gives the paragraph its structural form. If you glance at a page of any English text, you should be able to tell the number of paragraphs due to the fact that each of the paragraphs has been separated from the others by an indented line. Use the following format for your paragraphs:

1. Use 8.5" × 11" sized paper

2. Use 1" margins

3. Double space the paragraph

4. Include a title

5. Indent the first sentence of the paragraph

The following is a paragraph format. Note that the first line is indented, that is it starts a few spaces to the right. Also note that there are margins on either side of the paragraph.

Generating Ideas

Before you start writing, try to generate ideas you can use in your paragraph. This stage of paragraph development is important for a number of reasons. First of all, it allows you to jot down your ideas on paper or on a computer. Secondly, ideas do not usually come in a logically sequenced way that is suitable for a paragraph. Ideas tend to come in bits and pieces, and your task as a writer is to put them in complete thoughts and rearrange them to form a coherent paragraph. It is easier to do all these on paper or on a computer than in your mind.

There are many ways to gather ideas. One way is to write freely on your topic for as long as the ideas stream out of your head. This initial piece usually includes useful ideas as well as ideas you may not need to write the first draft of your paragraph. Another way to generate ideas is to list words or phrases pertaining to the topic. These can then be categorized and a paragraph can be developed by using the ideas in each category.

The Topic Sentence

The topic sentence is a very important part of the paragraph. A topic sentence has two parts: the topic and the controlling idea. The topic is the subject of the paragraph and the controlling idea expresses your opinion, attitude, or an idea about the subject. Controlling ideas are not facts about the topic. They are judgmental terms that have to be supported with facts, statistics, quotations, etc. The controlling idea not only helps you stay focused but also allows you to support your opinion.

Make sure that your topic sentence:
    a. is a complete sentence.
    b. expresses an idea or an opinion.
    c. is not too general.
    d. is not too specific.
    e. has a controlling idea.
    f. can be supported.

TASK   Read the following topic sentences. Put a check next to the good topic sentences. Be ready to explain why the others are not good topic sentences.

1. _____ Mary is a hardworking person.
2. _____ Regular Coca-Cola has caffeine.
3. _____ Mary has red hair.
4. _____ The president of the United States lives in the White House.
5. _____ My room is messy.
6. _____ He is a good student.
7. _____ The students in this class can be classified into three groups.
8. _____ A community college is a two-year post secondary institution.
9. _____ I like my neighborhood.
10. _____ Doctors take a number of steps to diagnose a disease.
11. _____ Traffic accidents can be caused by inattentive drivers.
12. _____ He has a gorgeous house.
13. _____ The two education systems are similar in many ways.
14. _____ I take issue with arranged marriages.

Support Sentences

The majority of the sentences in a paragraph are support sentences. The reason for this is that it is easy to express an opinion, but it may take a lot of ideas to convince others to accept your point of view. Unlike the topic sentence, which states an idea or an opinion, support sentences state facts, explain, give examples, illustrate, and describe people, events, or places in support of an opinion. They may also report ideas from reliable sources.

Because you are trying to support an assertion, not only do you need enough convincing support sentences, but the way those sentences are presented in your paragraph is also important. For instance, you may begin with the least convincing, systematically present your supporting ideas, and end with the most convincing. Furthermore, the support sentences have to be in logical order.

Make sure that all your support sentences:

    a.   are complete sentences.

    b.   support the controlling idea of the topic sentence.

    c.   are convincing.

    d.   are in logical order.

    e.   are grammatically connected.

Unity

All the sentences in a paragraph are about a single idea often introduced in the topic sentence. The sentences in the body of a paragraph have the same purpose: they support the main idea. As for the concluding sentence, it may restate the main idea, summarize the supporting ideas, or make a relevant closing remark. If all the sentences in a paragraph are closely connected by their reference and relevance to the main idea, then the paragraph has unity.

Sentences that do not belong in a paragraph destroy the unity of the paragraph. The controlling idea in the topic sentence is a good determining factor to test relevance. If a sentence does not support the controlling idea, it is irrelevant, and disrupts the flow of the paragraph. As the word "controlling" suggests, the controlling idea forces the writer to stick to the idea being developed.

TASK   Below is a topic sentence with a list of support sentences. Cross out the ones you don't consider good support sentences and give your reason. You may use the above list of criteria for a good support sentence to help you make your decision.

Topic sentence: My trip to the U.S. was full of surprises.

Support sentences: 1.   My flight was delayed for five hours.

                      2.   I was sitting next to a friend I hadn't seen for years.

                      3.   The food wasn't what I expected.

                      4.   The food was cold and looked unappetizing.

                      5.   A flight attendant surprised me with a gift.

                      6.   As expected, I was met at the airport by my host family.

7. I pretended to be surprised.

8. I had to pay for my drinks.

9. I was shocked when my host family greeted me in my language.

10. The flight attendants were very courteous.

11. The trip took longer than I expected.

12. Members of my host family spoke my language fluently.

Coherence

All the sentences in the body of a paragraph must not only be related to the topic sentence, but they must also be in logical order. Incoherence is what makes a listener or reader think twice about the speaker or writer's thought process or even sanity. Let us say your teacher walks up to the front of the class and says, "My name is John Doe. I teach English as a Second Language. I had a good breakfast this morning. I drive a Honda. I am delighted you are taking this class." You may come to the conclusion that something is wrong with the teacher. Your reason for reaching such a conclusion is because he is not coherent. As you sit there, you are probably wondering how or whether these ideas are logically connected. A reader may have a similar reaction when he or she reads a paragraph that lacks coherence.

Some steps are naturally ordered. For instance, when a seed is sown, it germinates, becomes a plant and eventually turns into a tree. The ordering of these steps is a given. However, the ordering of ideas in a paragraph is not usually as obvious. As a writer, you have to figure out the order you want your ideas to be in your paragraph.

There are many ways to make your paragraphs coherent. For instance, doing an outline and rearranging the ideas so that they are in logical order is one way to make sure that there is coherence.

TASK The support sentences in the task under unity above are not in logical order. The sentences, for example, can be ordered according to the time they occurred. Put the relevant support sentences in the appropriate category.

A: **Before the flight**	B: **During the flight**	C: **After the flight**
_____	_____	_____
_____	_____	_____
_____	_____	_____
_____	_____	_____

Can you think of another way to rearrange the ideas so that they are coherent?

Another way is to use tenses, connectors such as coordinators, subordinators, and conjunctive adverbs for coherence in your writing. The sentences below, for example, do not seem to be in logical order; however, by using conjunctions, one can connect them in such a way that the ideas flow or are logically connected. Below the list of sentences, see how the ideas are connected to form a coherent sentence.

I studied English in my country.

I was able to communicate with Americans.

I came to the U.S. in 1995.

I was glad I studied English in my country.

I was glad I **had studied** English in my country, **for** I was able to communicate with Americans **when** I came to the U.S. in 1995.

With the past perfect tense (had studied), and connectors (for and when), the sentences have been logically connected. The past perfect tense **"had studied"** shows that the writer's studying English occurred before he was glad about the action he took. Secondly, the coordinator **"for"** connects the cause, studying English in his country and the result, which is that he was able to communicate with Americans. The subordinator **"when"** connects what he was able to do and when he did it.

The Concluding Sentence

The concluding sentence is where a writer signals and then brings the paragraph to an end. Words or phrases used to signal the end include the following: finally, to sum up, in conclusion, as you can see. These "signal words or phrases" usually begin the concluding sentence and are followed by a comma. The concluding sentence must not be indented like the topic sentence.

What concluding sentence you choose to use in a paragraph depends on the kind of paragraph you are writing. For example, a restatement of the topic sentence may be a good concluding sentence for a paragraph developed by examples whereas a statement indicating result may be the best conclusion for a process paragraph. For example, if the topic sentence of a paragraph reads: "My trip to the museum was instructive," a restatement as a concluding sentence may be: "I learned a lot during my visit to the museum."

A suitable concluding sentence for a cause and effect paragraph, however, is a statement that suggests how to prevent or maintain the effect depending on whether or not it is desirable. For example, a concluding sentence of a paragraph on traffic accidents may be a statement of what has to be done to avoid accidents. On the other hand, a paragraph that discusses the causes of good health calls for a concluding sentence that states how to maintain good health. Other concluding sentences are in the form of a summary. Use this kind of conclusion to remind your readers of the ideas presented in the body of the paragraph. Yet another kind of conclusion is a comment, or a statement that looks to the future given what has been presented in the paragraph.

Make sure that your concluding sentence:

a. is a complete sentence.

b. is suitable for the paragraph you are writing.

c. is a paraphrase of the topic sentence if you choose to restate the main idea.

d. is not indented.

TASK   Read the following topic sentences and the pair of concluding sentences that follows each and decide which of them is better.

1. Topic sentence: Public colleges and universities classify students as in-state or out-of-state.

    Concluding sentences:

    _____ I am an out-of-state student.

    _____ Students in public colleges and universities are classified as in-state or out-of-state.

2. Topic sentence: I like my neighborhood.

    Concluding sentences:

    _____ To sum up, I like where I live because it is quiet, clean, and convenient.

    _____ The neighborhood is in Fairfax County.

3. Topic sentence: Registering for this class is a multi-step process.

    Concluding sentences:

    _____ If you successfully complete this process, you will

    have registered for the class.

    _____ There is another way you can register, but I would rather not get into that.

4. Topic sentence: Traffic accidents can be caused by drivers who are speeding.

    Concluding sentences:

    _____ If people drive within the speed limit, there will be fewer accidents.

    _____ Pedestrians should avoid jaywalking.

5. Topic sentence: The party was a disaster.

    Concluding sentences:

    _____ As you can see one mishap led to the other.

    _____ The music was good.

6. Topic sentence: A rotary phone and a cellular phone differ in many ways.

   Concluding sentences:

   _____ In conclusion, due to its size, mobility, and convenience, the cellular phone has become more popular than the rotary phone.

   _____ Cellular phones cause accidents.

7. Topic sentence: I take issue with arranged marriages.

   Concluding sentences:

   _____ My parents had an arranged marriage.

   _____ I am against arranged marriages.

The Complete Sentence

A paragraph is made of sentences. All the sentences in a paragraph must be complete. That is to say, they must have a subject, verb, and express a complete thought. As you may have realized, that a sentence be complete is one of the criteria listed for the topic sentence, support sentences, and concluding sentence of a paragraph.

Fragments or incomplete sentences do not express complete thoughts. Even though fragments are common in speech, they should be avoided in writing. For example, a disappointed sister who was looking forward to having some pie and found out that her brother ate it may ask, "Why did you eat my pie?" To which the brother may answer: "Because I was hungry." The brother's answer is understood, but when written by itself, it doesn't express a complete thought. It is a dependent clause and cannot stand by itself.

It is important to make sure that all the sentences in your paragraphs are complete. Make sure that each sentence has a subject, a verb or complete verb phrase, and that it expresses a complete thought. One way to know whether or not a sentence expresses a complete thought is to see if you can answer all reasonable clarification questions about the sentence. See examples below.

Examples   **Complete sentence: *John ate the pie.***

Questions	**Answers**
What did John eat?	John ate the pie.
Who ate the pie?	John did.
What happened to the pie?	John ate it.
Where is the pie?	It is in John's stomach.

Incomplete sentence: *After John ate the pie.*

Questions	**Answers**
What did John eat?	John ate the pie.
Who ate the pie?	John did.
What happened to the pie?	John ate it.
Where is the pie?	It's in John's stomach.
What happened after John ate the pie?	We don't know.

It is possible to give answers to the first set of questions because they are about a complete sentence that has a complete thought. However, we can't give the answer to the last question in the second set because the clause does not express a complete thought. We need new information to answer this question.

Other common fragments are a result of incomplete verb phrases. All the progressive, perfect, and future tenses have helping verbs or auxiliaries in addition to the main verb. Without these auxiliaries, the verb phrase is incomplete thus the sentence is a fragment.

Examples

He **going** home.

I **come** to the meeting tomorrow.

I already **done** the assignment.

The main verb in each of the sentences above needs an auxiliary, without which the sentence is a fragment. The main verb in the first sentence is in the progressive form; as a result, it must be used with the auxiliary "**be.**" The main verb in the second sentence needs the auxiliary "**will**" for the future tense, and the verb in the third sentence has to have the auxiliary "**have**" for the perfect tense.

TASK 1 Correct the following fragments. What is missing in each fragment is an auxiliary or helping verb.

1. I doing my homework.

2. I be there tomorrow.

3. I been living in the United States since August, 1995.

4. I been in this country for five years.

5. He going to work.

6. I already seen that movie.

7. I will going back to work next week.

8. I taking ESL at a community college.

Phrases and Clauses

A combination of words does not necessarily make a complete sentence. A group of words can be a phrase, a dependent clause, or an independent clause. It is important to be able to identify an independent clause and better yet, a dependent clause and a phrase, for as fragments, if they appear in your draft, you have to correct them.

Examples

1. The lady in the blue dress.   (Phrase)
2. Studying and working full-time.   (Phrase)
3. Because I was hungry.   (Dependent clause)
4. While I was waiting for the bus.   (Dependent clause)
5. I ate the pizza.   (Independent Clause)

TASK 2 Decide whether each of the numbered groups of words is a phrase, dependent clause, or independent clause.

1. When I got home.
   _____ Phrase
   _____ Dependent clause
   _____ Independent clause

2. Due to the fact that I was tired.
   _____ Phrase
   _____ Dependent clause
   _____ Independent clause

3. I was exhausted.
   _____ Phrase
   _____ Dependent clause
   _____ Independent clause

4. Standing next to the blackboard.
   _____ Phrase
   _____ Dependent clause
   _____ Independent clause

5. The man talking to the student.
   _____ Phrase
   _____ Dependent clause
   _____ Independent clause

6. My English as a Second Language class that meets in the morning.
   _____ Phrase
   _____ Dependent clause
   _____ Independent clause

7. My English as a Second Language class meets in the morning.
   _____ Phrase
   _____ Dependent clause
   _____ Independent clause

8. Come home as soon as possible.
   _____ Phrase
   _____ Dependent clause
   _____ Independent clause

9. At the back of the class.
   _____ Phrase
   _____ Dependent clause
   _____ Independent clause

10. Where can I sit?
    _____ Phrase
    _____ Dependent clause
    _____ Independent clause

11. That bothers me.
    _____ Phrase
    _____ Dependent clause
    _____ Independent clause

12. That he has not paid his rent bothers me.
    _____ Phrase
    _____ Dependent clause
    _____ Independent clause

13. Having done his assignment.
    _____ Phrase
    _____ Dependent clause
    _____ Independent clause

14. He'd done his homework.
    _____ Phrase
    _____ Dependent clause
    _____ Independent clause

15. By the time he comes home.
    _____ Phrase
    _____ Dependent clause
    _____ Independent clause

16. He will have done his assignment.
    _____ Phrase
    _____ Dependent clause
    _____ Independent clause

17. By the time he came, I had already made dinner.
    _____ Phrase
    _____ Dependent clause
    _____ Independent clause

18. Please be quiet.
    _____ Phrase
    _____ Dependent clause
    _____ Independent clause

19. Send it first class.
    _____ Phrase
    _____ Dependent clause
    _____ Independent clause

20. Sit.
_____ Phrase
_____ Dependent clause
_____ Independent clause

TASK 3 Carefully read each of the following groups of words and decide whether or not it is a complete sentence. If you find a fragment, fix it by providing what you think is missing.

1. Being a foreign student.

   _____

2. Out of state tuition.

   _____

3. I am a full-time student.

   _____

4. When I was in my country.

   _____

5. That he is an out of state student.

   _____

6. Foreign student orientation.

   _____

7. Counselors at this college are helpful.

   _____

8. Be nice to him.

   _____

9. In order to be considered an in-state student.

   _____

10. You must live in the state for at least one year.

   _____

11. He is a good student.

   _____

12. Why do you think he is a good student?

   _____

13. I have no idea.

   _____

14. Be there on time.

   _____

Non-Idiomatic Sentences or Awkward Sentences

Students often write sentences that do not sound like English even though they may have a subject, verb, and the potential to convey a complete thought. Usually, the problem is that the sentences do not have the English word order, i.e. S V O (subject, verb, and object). A common practice by second language learners is to think in their native language, which may have a different word order, and then translate their thoughts into English. Such a process almost always produces awkward or non-idiomatic sentences. English is an S V O language; however, other languages may be V S O, O S V, or V O S. English word order may differ from that of other languages as shown below.

English: I like rice. (SVO)

Chinese: 我 喜欢 米饭。 (SVO)

Korean: 나는 밥을 좋아한다. (SOV)

Japanese: 私 は ごはん が 好きです。 (SOV)

Arabic: أحبُّ الرزَّ (VSO)

Wolof: Man bëgg naa ceeb. (SVO)

Vietnamese: Tôi thích cỏm. (SVO)

Farsi: من برنج را دوست دارم (SOV)

Even though English is referred to as an SVO language, there are a number of sentence patterns that are used in English. The basic sentence structure, however, is subject + predicate. The subject is the topic of the sentence and the predicate comments on the subject; in other words, the predicate tells us, among other things, what the subject is, what it did, what happened to it, or where it went or is going. The following are sentence structures that are commonly used in English:

	Subject	predicate	
1.	John	left.	(S V)
2.	Kim	drinks coffee.	(S V O)
3.	Sam	is diligent.	(S V C)
4.	Mary	studies at home.	(S V Prep phrase)
5.	Charlotte	is my teacher.	(S V Noun phrase)
6.	I	gave her my assignment.	S V O (indirect) O (direct)
7.	I	gave my assignment to her.	S V O (direct) O (indirect)
8.	I	had my friend review my paper.	S V (causative) O V (base form or infinitive) O

As you can see in the sentences above, the predicate can be in different forms ranging from a verb that simply states an action to one that is followed by two objects, direct and indirect, or a causative verb that is followed by a structure that has an object of the initial clause and another verb and an object.

TASK 4 Put each group of words in the correct order to form a correct sentence structure.

1. In front of my apartment a bus stop is there.

   _____

2. Clean my neighborhood is.

   _____

3. Friendly are my neighbors.

   _____

4. Quiet in a neighborhood I live.

   _____

5. I convenient live in a neighborhood.

   _____

6. I find always a space parking.

   _____

7. Is safe my neighborhood.

   _____

8. Always greet me my neighbors.

   _____

9. Many banks are there in my neighborhood.

_____

10. Shoppers Food Warehouse just two blocks is from my apartment.

_____

ENABLING GRAMMAR EXERCISES

SUBJECTS

The subject of a sentence can be a noun (proper noun, pronoun, common noun, count noun, non-count noun), phrase, or clause. It can also be singular or plural.

Washington D.C. is the capital of the United States. (Proper noun—place)

Charlotte is our ESL teacher. (Proper noun—person)

John and Mary are classmates. (plural proper nouns)

The book is on the shelf. (Common, count noun)

Traffic is always heavy. (Non-count noun)

The chairs are in the classroom. (Plural common noun)

The lady in the red shirt is my sister. (Phrase)

That he fails all his exams worries me. (Clause)

The subject of each of the sentences above can be replaced by a subject pronoun.

Subject Pronouns

	First person	Second person	Third person
Singular	I	You	He / She / It
Plural	We	You	They

EXERCISE 1   Give the corresponding pronoun for each of the following nouns or noun phrases.

Example: My friends <u>They</u>_____

1. My parents _____

2. My family _____

3. The cars _____

4. My rent_____

5. The United States _____

6. Virginia and Maryland _____

7. Traffic _____

8. Disabled cars _____

9. The police _____

10. Police officers _____

11. A policeman _____

12. The audience _____

13. The crowd _____

14. The students _____

15. A group of students _____

16. Three groups of students _____

17. Few students _____

18. Kim _____

19. Kim, Mike, and I _____

20. You and Janet _____

EXERCISE 2   Underline the subject and state whether it can be replaced by a singular or plural, first, second or third person pronoun.

Example: *Studying English* is fun. (singular, third person)

1. My family lives in Seoul.

2. Citizens of my country are proud to host the Olympics.

3. Members of my family are close to each other.

4. Studying full-time and working part-time is not easy.

5. My sister loves rock music.

6. The United States has many large cities.

7. My sister and I are twins.

8. Both of us rely on our parents.

9. The computer is a useful machine.

10. Traffic is heavy during rush hour.

11. The furniture in my room belongs to my brother.

12. A coffee table, two chairs, and a sofa are all I have in my apartment.

13. Each state has a capital.

14. Most of the students in my class are immigrants.

15. Every student in my class speaks at least two languages.

16. Each of the states in the U.S. has a capital.

Linking Verbs and Action Verbs

Linking verbs connect subjects and complements, which may be a noun or an adjective. If the complement is a noun, the subject and the noun are co-referents. In other words, the subject and the noun that comes after the linking verb refer to each other. If the complement is an adjective, it, the predicate adjective, modifies the subject.

Example: Charlotte is our ESL teacher.

The verb — be (is) links the subject — "Charlotte" — to the predicate — "is our ESL teacher."

There are other verbs that link subjects and their complement. These verbs act like the linking verb **be** in that they connect the subject to another noun that refers to the subject or an adjective that modifies it. These verbs include: look, seem, appear, taste, smell, become, remain, etc. See the list in the box below. Some of these verbs, however, may be used as action verbs as indicated in the following example.

Example: He remained president. (Linking)
               He remained in his room. (Action)

Linking Verbs		
appear	be	become
fall	feel	grow
look	remain	seem
smell	sound	stand
stay	taste	

EXERCISE 3   Use the given information and an appropriate linking verb of your choice to form sentences. Make sure that each sentence has a subject, a linking verb, and a complement noun or adjective.

1. People / old

_____

2. The music / good

_____

3. The patient / better

_____

4. The cake / delicious

_____

5. The patient / worse

_____

6. The immigrant / a citizen

_____

7. The assignment / difficult

_____

8. His accent / beautiful

_____

9. James / my brother

_____

10. My homework / easy

_____

11. My sister / married

_____

12. My brother / a married man

_____

13. All animals / old

_____

14. The pizza / stale

_____

15. The incense / good

_____

Action Verbs

Action verbs show movement whereas linking verbs describe a state or condition.

Examples:

The football player looks tired.   (Linking)

The football player looks for his helmet.   (Action)

There are as many action verbs as the number of movements that can be made. Think of all the movements you can make as you sit where you are. You can stand, talk, write, close your eyes, raise your hand, etc. The words that indicate all these movements are action verbs.

EXERCISE 4   Underline the verb in each of the following sentences and state the type of verb it is, i.e., linking or action.

1. He looks good.

2. The football player appears tired.

3. The football player looked for his car keys.

4. We are the audience.

5. The students are frustrated.

6. He seems to know the answer.

7. He looks tired.

8. The perfume smells good.

9. People grow old.

10. Children grow up.

11. The assignment seems difficult.

12. He became a grandfather.

13. Cooks always taste the food they make.

14. Athletes stay healthy.

15. The athlete stayed home.

16. He is the teacher.

17. He is in his office.

18. I feel better.

19. Jazz music sounds good.

20. The bell sounds for the service to begin.

21. He stands alone.

22. I stand corrected.

23. She stands all day.

24. The coffee tastes good.

25. He tasted the wine.

TRANSITIVE AND INTRANSITIVE VERBS

Action verbs can be further divided into two kinds: **Transitive** and **Intransitive.**

Transitive verbs are action verbs that need an object. In other words, the action is done to somebody or something. Intransitive verbs, on the other hand, do not take an object; the action simply takes place.

Examples

He baked the cake.   (Bake—transitive)

She slept.   (Sleep—intransitive)

EXERCISE 5   Indicate whether the verb in each sentence is transitive or intransitive.

1. He formed an organization.

2. The group met.

3. He drinks coffee.

4. He drinks.

5. He drives an SUV.

6. The car drives well.

7. Mary is expecting a guest.

8. Mary is expecting.

9. She put the baby to sleep.

10. The baby slept all day.

SUBJECT–VERB AGREEMENT

If the subject of the sentence is a third person singular noun or pronoun, an **s** is added to the base form of the verb. All other subject nouns and pronouns take the base form in the simple present tense.

1. I **like** apples.

2. He **likes** apples.

3. We **drink** coffee.

4. She **drinks** coffee.

5. You **live** in a small town.

6. She **lives** in a small town.

7. They **do** their homework in the library. / She does her homework in the library

8. We **study** at home.   She studies at home

9. He **uses** the computer everyday.

10. It **rises** in the east and **sets** in the west.

EXERCISE 6   Knowing the subject of a sentence helps in determining whether or not the verb takes an -s. Underline the subject in each of the following sentences.

1. I go to the movies once a week.

2. We go to the movies once in a blue moon.

3. You seldom go to the movies.

4. She goes to the movies every now and then.

5. He rarely goes to the movies.

6. They never go to the movies.

7. Being an immigrant is not easy.

8. Most of my classmates are new immigrants.

9. Some English as a Second Language students experience culture shock.

10. Almost all of the students in my class speak more than one language.

EXERCISE 7   Complete the following sentences with the appropriate form of one of the given verbs.

listen   know   play   go   like   write   enjoy

1. I _____ play _____ soccer.
2. He _____ plays _____ baseball.
3. We _____ enjoy _____ camping.
4. They _____ listen _____ classical music.
5. You _____ like _____ being alone.
6. I _ Know _ how to ride a bike.
7. He _____ knows _____ how to get there.
8. We _____ know _____ his name.
9. She _____ writes _____ my phone number.
10. They _____ know _____ what he likes for Christmas.
11. I _____ listen _____ to music.
12. She _____ goes _____ to jazz music.
13. She _____ goes _____ to the radio.
14. He _ likes _ to his parents.
15. They do not _ know what he says _ to the teacher.

EXERCISE 8   Complete the sentence with the simple present tense of the verb in parenthesis.

1. I _____ come _____ (come) from Vietnam.
2. My sister _____ works _____ (work) full-time.
3. I _____ am _____ (be) an immigrant.
4. He _____ goes _____ (go) to Northern Virginia Community College.
5. We _____ prefer _____ (prefer) pizza.
6. He _____ disturbs _____ (disturb) me.
7. Seoul _____ is _____ (be) a big city.
8. My dad _____ wakes _____ (wake) me up every morning.
9. Northern Virginia Community College _____ has _____ (have) six campuses.
10. One of the campuses _____ is _____ (be) in Manassas.
11. Annandale _____ is _____ (be) my home campus.
12. He _____ speaks _____ (speak) Spanish.
13. She _____ writes _____ (write) good paragraphs.
14. I _____ take _____ (take) the bus to school.
15. One of my friends _____ goes _____ (go) to school after work.

16. Almost all of my friends _____work_____ (work) full-time.
17. One of my classmates _____works_____ (work) at McDonald's.
18. He _____talks_____ (talk) too much.
19. We seldom _____eat_____ (eat) out.
20. Washington D.C. _____is_____ (be) the capital of the United States.

EXERCISE 9   Fill in the blanks with an appropriate verb in the simple present tense.

1. The sun _____rises_____ in the east.
2. My family _____lives_____ in Fairfax, Virginia.
3. ESL _____is_____ English as a Second Language.
4. The tuition at Northern Virginia Community College _____is_____ reasonable.
5. The sun _____set_____ in the west.
6. I always _____pay_____ for my classes online.
7. My sister _____pays_____ for her classes in person; she _____is_____ talking on the phone. As a matter of fact, when the phone _____rings_____ at home, she never _____take_____ it.
8. I _____visit_____ my parents, who are in my country, once a week.
9. I _____go_____ to bed at 10 o'clock.
10. It _____is_____ now 8 o'clock.
11. I always _____review_____ my grammar, spelling, and punctuation before I _____hand over_____ my paragraph to the teacher.
12. My friend _____writes_____ good paragraphs.
13. She always _____read_____ her rough draft.
14. He always _____asks_____ to get help from the teacher.

EDITING

It is important to read over your rough draft and correct the mistakes you find. Some students believe that it is the teacher's duty to find the mistakes and point them out to the student or even correct them for the student. You are supposed to edit your paragraph before you hand it in. Editing makes your paragraph look and sound better.

If you know what your problems are, you should first concentrate on those problems when you edit. For example, if you usually make subject/verb agreement mistakes, you should carefully read your paragraph, underline every subject, circle every verb, and make sure the subjects agree with their verbs. If spelling is your problem, get a dictionary and look up the words you don't think you spelled correctly. Do not rely on spell check, for you may have the correct spelling of a word, but it might not be the word you need. Read your paragraph over as many times as the number of mistakes you usually make.

The following paragraph has subject/verb agreement mistakes. Correct all the mistakes you can find.

I like my neighborhood because it is convenient, safe, and clean. First of all, there are a shopping center in my neighborhood where I can find banks, grocery stores, a CVS, a gas station, and the list go on. I don't have to go far to do my shopping or banking. It is also close to I-66, a highway that run east to Washington and west to Manassas and beyond. In addition, my neighborhood is safe. The police patrols the neighborhood day and night. We also have a neighborhood watch. The neighbors calls the police if they see a stranger in the neighborhood. Last but not the least, my neighborhood is very clean. People cleans their yard and mows the grass once every week. No one litter. The trash are picked up every Thursday. This is the cleanest neighborhood I have ever lived in. I really like my neighborhood; I think I will stay in the neighborhood as long as I live in the United States.

EXERCISE 10   This paragraph was written by a low intermediate ESL student. The student's main problem seems to be tense consistency. Underline all the tenses and make them consistent.

My Life in the United States

My life in the United States is tiring. There are many reasons why my life in the United States is tiring. First of all, there are so many things I have to do before my day is over. I got up early in the morning every day Monday to Friday at about 6:00 A.M., helped my junior brothers get ready for school. After that, I took a shower and eat my breakfast. At about 9:00 A.M., I catch a bus to school. My bus ride to school is about an hour, and some days, I felt so tired that I even slept in the bus. I spent four hours in school, then do the same routine of bus ride back home. At home, I do some cleaning, help my brothers with their homework and prepared the meal for everyone in the house. Then after that, I do my homework or do some reading before it is my bedtime. In fact, my whole day is so tiring that I always set my alarm clock every night in order to get up early the next day.

E. A.

PARAGRAPH ANALYSIS

EXERCISE 11   Read the following sample paragraph and answer the questions that follow.

My friend, Yu is hard working. He works in a restaurant. He works seven days a week. Every day, he comes to the restaurant at 10:30 A.M. even though the restaurant opens at 11:00 A.M. What does he do? He prepares the food and does anything he can. Sometimes when the other workers can't come to work, he helps do their job. Every day when the workers take turns to eat lunch, he is always the last to eat lunch. Sometimes when the restaurant has some special orders before business time, he will come to help even though that is not his job. When the restaurant closes, he helps to clean up. Yu likes to work. He is a diligent employee.

1. Does the paragraph begin with an indented line?   Yes

2. Does the paragraph have a topic sentence?

3. Where in the paragraph is the topic sentence?

4. Does the topic sentence have a controlling idea?

5. How many supporting ideas does the writer give?

6. Are the supporting ideas relevant?

7. Are the supporting ideas convincing?

8. Is there a conclusion?

9. Is the conclusion a restatement of the topic sentence?

10. Are there margins on both sides of the paragraph?

UNIT ONE
Example

OBJECTIVES

By the end of this unit, you should be able:

- ■ to construct the topic sentence, support sentences, and concluding sentence of an example paragraph

- ■ to determine relevant ideas in support of the controlling idea of an example paragraph on a topic with which you are familiar

- ■ to use simple present tense and determiners

- ■ to compose and edit a rough draft of an example paragraph

---

PART I: THE EXAMPLE PARAGRAPH

In a paragraph developed by examples, you have to provide reasons or examples to support the opinion you have put forth in your topic sentence, which is the main idea of the paragraph. As a rule, a topic sentence has a controlling idea. In other words, it includes a thought that has to be supported by examples. Remember that some people may disagree with you, or others may not fully accept your point of view. Therefore, you have to come up with examples to convince them. For instance, if you claim to be a *good* student, you should have enough examples to back your assertion that you are *good*, which is the controlling idea. Likewise, if you accuse someone of doing something, you had better have convincing proof that the person is the culprit.

A paragraph developed by examples needs relevant support sentences. In other words, your examples have to be related to the topic. For instance, in trying to convince someone that you are a good student, it doesn't help to say that you are six feet tall and weigh two hundred pounds. Your height and weight have nothing to do with being a good student. This information is totally irrelevant to the issue in question. Irrelevant support sentences destroy paragraph unity.

Furthermore, a sentence may be relevant but not convincing. To say you are a good student because you always sit in the front may be a relevant supporting idea, but it is not quite convincing. After all, some students may sit in the front of a class, yet they are not necessarily good students. It is important to note that you are trying to convince others to accept your opinion; you do not want to give them reason to think otherwise.

Besides being relevant and convincing, you need to have enough support sentences. Students often ask what the minimum or maximum number of examples in a paragraph is. There is no specific number that is required. The number depends on the point you are trying to prove and how strong your examples are. For instance, if a person is caught red handed, it may not be necessary to dwell on suspicious behavior. However, to convince people that a suspect who looks innocent is actually guilty, it may be necessary to have as many convincing reasons as possible.

Yet another important consideration in writing an example paragraph is the order in which the support sentences appear in the text. They may be ordered chronologically; that is, in sequence by time of occurrence. Support sentences in an example paragraph may also begin with the weakest examples and end with the strongest support sentences. When you end with your best example, the reader is left convinced.

In this unit, you will work on writing paragraphs developed by examples.

Activity 1.1

Paragraph Analysis

TASK The following paragraph was written by a student in a low-intermediate ESL program. Read the paragraph and answer the questions that follow.

My Life in the United States

My life in the United States is very busy. In fact, I am a full-time student, and I have a full-time job. I always wake up early in the morning to go to school. I even don't have enough time to eat breakfast. After school, I have a hurried lunch in the cafeteria and go to work immediately. I usually return home from work after 8:00 p.m. I often stay up late at night to do my homework. I am busy not only on weekdays but also on weekends. I often spend much time doing housework. Every weekend, I have to clean my house, do the laundry, and go food shopping. I also spend time doing charity work at a nursing home every Sunday. I don't have any time for relaxation. In conclusion, I am always very tired because I have a lot of things to do during the week.

C. Nguyen

1. Does the paragraph have a topic sentence?
2. Does the topic sentence have a controlling idea?
3. Does the paragraph have enough support sentences?
4. Are all the support sentences relevant? Do they support the controlling idea?
5. Are the support sentences convincing?
6. How are the support sentences ordered?
7. Does the paragraph have a conclusion?
8. What kind of conclusion is it?

Example   **27**

PART II: ELEMENTS OF AN EXAMPLE PARAGRAPH

Activity 1.2

The Topic Sentence of an Example Paragraph

The topic sentence of an example paragraph is usually a statement that expresses the writer's opinion about the subject. Remember, a topic sentence has two parts: the topic and the controlling idea, which is your opinion about the topic. A good topic sentence usually has the following criteria:

1. It has a topic and controlling idea.
2. It is a sentence that expresses an opinion or an idea.
3. It is a complete sentence.
4. It is not a factual statement.
5. It is not too general and not too specific.
6. It is supportable.

TASK 1   Read the following sentences carefully and decide whether or not they are good topic sentences. Give your reasons if you think a sentence is not a good topic sentence.

1. My neighborhood is three miles from downtown.

   Can this be a topic sentence? _____ Yes

   _____ No   (Why not) _____

2. My neighborhood has good schools.

   Can this be a topic sentence? _____ Yes

   _____ No   (Why not) _____

3. I like my neighborhood.

   Can this be a topic sentence? _____ Yes

   _____ No   (Why not) _____

4. My neighborhood is noisy.

   Can this be a topic sentence? _____ Yes

   _____ No   (Why not) _____

5. My neighborhood has people of different nationalities.

   Can this be a topic sentence? _____ Yes

   _____ No   (Why not) _____

6. My neighborhood has a dumpster.

   Can this be a topic sentence? _____ Yes

   _____ No (Why not) _____

7. My neighborhood has many recreation centers.

   Can this be a topic sentence? _____ Yes

   _____ No (Why not) _____

8. My neighborhood is next to a highway.

   Can this be a topic sentence? _____ Yes

   _____ No (Why not) _____

9. Is my neighborhood clean?

   Can this be a topic sentence? _____ Yes

   _____ No (Why not) _____

10. My neighborhood has a high school.

    Can this be a topic sentence? _____ Yes

    _____ No (Why not) _____

11. People of different nationalities who live in my neighborhood.

    Can this be a topic sentence? _____ Yes

    _____ No (Why not) _____

TASK 2 Write a topic sentence on each of the following topics. You may use the criteria of a good topic sentence listed on page 27.

1. Your class
2. Your family
3. A friend
4. One of your parents
5. Your school or language program

Example 29

Activity 1.3

Support Sentences

DETERMINING RELEVANT IDEAS

It is important to make sure that all your ideas are relevant; in other words, they are related to the topic and above all, they can be used to support the topic sentence. Irrelevant ideas interfere with coherence, the logical flow of the paragraph. These are the kinds of sentences that make the reader stop and wonder why they are in the paragraph.

TASK   Read the topic sentences below and cross out the support sentences that are irrelevant.

1. My neighborhood is convenient for my family.
   a. There is a shopping center in the neighborhood.
   b. There is a Laundromat two blocks from my house.
   c. We have a neighborhood watch.
   d. The bus stop is in front of my house.
   e. We moved here two years ago.
   f. My son walks to school.
   g. My parents live in the neighborhood.
   h. There are two hospitals within minutes from my house.
   i. The rent is affordable.

2. I like my neighborhood.
   a. It is quiet.
   b. There are people from my country in the neighborhood.
   c. It is clean.
   d. My children's friends live far from the neighborhood.
   e. The neighbors get along.
   f. There is a busy highway that goes through the neighborhood.
   g. My rent has been increased two years in a row.
   h. It is convenient.
   i. The lights on the highway that goes through the neighborhood are too bright.
   j. There are many recreation facilities.

3. I don't like this classroom.
   a. It is too cold in winter.
   b. It is too small.
   c. There is too much noise from the class next door.
   d. It is cozy.
   e. It is too hot in summer.
   f. There is no trash can in the room.
   g. The desks are too close to each other.
   h. The lighting is good enough.
   i. There is poor ventilation.

Activity 1.4

Detailing Support Sentences

Sometimes it may not be enough to simply state a support sentence; you may have to provide details to show why the idea is a good example to support the controlling idea of your paragraph. For example, if you like your neighborhood because it is accessible to public transportation, you might want to be more specific by stating the distance from your house to the nearest bus stop, metro station, or highway. Such details will clearly show accessibility.

TASK 1   Based on your experience, provide specific details for each of the support sentences below.

1.   Topic sentence: Fast food is very popular in the United States.

     Support sentence: There are many fast food restaurants in my neighborhood.

     Specific detail:

     _____

     _____

     Support sentence: People often have fast food for a meal.

     Specific detail:

     _____

     _____

2.   Topic sentence: A car is a necessity in the United States.

     Support sentence: I need a car to go grocery shopping.

     Specific detail:

     _____

     _____

     Support sentence: I cannot rely on public transportation.

     Specific detail:

     _____

     _____

Example   **31**

3. Topic sentence: International students have a lot to learn when they first arrive in the United States.

    Support sentence: They have to find a place to live.
    Specific detail:

    _____

    _____

    Support sentence: They need to know the public transportation system.
    Specific detail:

    _____

    _____

TASK 2 Write a topic sentence that expresses your opinion about each of the following topics, a support sentence, and provide specific details in support of your opinion.

1. Your family

    Topic sentence:

    Support sentence:

    Specific detail:

2. Your English language class.

    Topic sentence:

    Support sentence:

    Specific detail:

3. Shopping malls in the United States

    Topic sentence:

    Support sentence:

    Specific detail:

Activity 1.5

The Concluding Sentence

The concluding sentence of an example paragraph can be a restatement of the topic sentence, a prediction, a plan of action, a recommendation or a combination of two or more of these types of conclusions.

TASK   Carefully read the examples of conclusions below, which are for a paragraph about a neighborhood being culturally diverse; then write concluding sentences for each of the topic sentences that follow.

Example

Topic sentence: My neighborhood is culturally diverse.

Possible Concluding Sentences

My neighborhood has people of different nationalities. (Restatement)

As more immigrants move in, it is going to be even more culturally diverse. (Prediction)

I intend to learn about every culture represented in this neighborhood. (Plan of Action)

I highly recommend this neighborhood to people who like to experience different cultures. (Recommendation)

My neighborhood has people of different nationalities, so I highly recommend it to people who like to experience different cultures. (Combination)

1. I like my neighborhood.

   Restatement: _____

   _____

   Prediction: _____

   _____

   Plan of action: _____

   _____

   Recommendation:_____

   _____

   Combination: _____

   _____

2. Fast food is popular in the United States.

   Restatement: _____

   _____

Example   **33**

Prediction: _____

_____

Plan of action: _____

_____

Recommendation:_____

_____

Combination: _____

_____

3. International students have a lot to learn when they first arrive in the United States.

Restatement: _____

_____

Prediction: _____

_____

Plan of action: _____

_____

Recommendation:_____

_____

Combination: _____

_____

4. Shopping malls in the U.S. offer much more than merchandise.

Restatement: _____

_____

Prediction: _____

_____

Plan of action: _____

_____

Recommendation:_____

_____

Combination: _____

_____

PART III: WRITING YOUR EXAMPLE PARAGRAPH

Activity 1.6

Expressing an Opinion about a Topic

TASK   The following are topics about American culture. Now that you have lived in the U.S. for some time, you must have an opinion about some or all of the topics below. Write a statement that expresses your opinion about each of the following. Share your opinion with other members of the class.

Example

Topic: American eating habits

Opinion: Americans eat anywhere and at any time.

1. Topic: Transportation in your area

    Your opinion: _____

    _____

    _____

2. Topic: Life in the U.S.

    Your opinion: _____

    _____

    _____

3. Topic: Shopping malls

    Your opinion: _____

    _____

    _____

4. Topic: Your neighborhood

    Your opinion: _____

    _____

    _____

5. Topic: Food shopping in the U.S.

    Your opinion: _____

    _____

    _____

Example   **35**

Activity 1.7

Generating Ideas to Support an Opinion

The opinions you have expressed about the topics above may have been based on intuition, an expression of how you feel without thinking about it. On the other hand, they may have been the result of careful observations of things and activities, or facts you have come across. For example, you may have the feeling that your neighborhood is quiet without thinking about why it is quiet. On the other hand, you may have noticed that there are a number of places such as banks, shops, recreation centers, and places of worship close to your house; as a result, you may come to the conclusion that you live in a convenient neighborhood. In any case, if you make an assertion in a topic sentence, you must come up with examples to support your opinion.

TASK 1 The following list was made during a brainstorming activity. The students were asked to state what they would want in a neighborhood. The items were listed as they were sounded off by the students. Add what you would want in a neighborhood to the list.

_____	Transportation	_____	Clean
_____	Safe	_____	Quiet
_____	Post office	_____	Diversity
_____	Playground	_____	Church
_____	Dumpster	_____	Hospital
_____	Convenience	_____	Laundromat
_____	School	_____	Fast food
_____	Metro station	_____	McDonald's
_____	Bus stop	_____	Shopping center
_____	People of my nationality	_____	Parents
_____	Entertainment	_____	_____
_____	Educated people	_____	_____
_____	Gas station	_____	_____
_____	People who are busy	_____	_____
_____	Club	_____	_____

Prioritizing Ideas

TASK 2 Number the items in order of importance. In other words, put (1) next to the item you think is the most important for you to have in a neighborhood, (2) next to the second most important and so on. Compare your priority lists. Discuss your reasons for listing certain items high or low.

TASK 3 List your top ten items you would like in a neighborhood.

1. _____
2. _____
3. _____
4. _____
5. _____
6. _____
7. _____
8. _____
9. _____
10. _____

TASK 4 Identify other words from the list that can be used as controlling ideas of a topic sentence about a neighborhood and add them to the following list.

1. Safe
2. Convenient
3. _____
4. _____
5. _____
6. _____
7. _____

Does one of these words describe how you feel about your neighborhood? If not, can you think of another word that best describes your opinion about your neighborhood?

Example   **37**

TASK 5 Complete the following topic sentence. You may use one of the words above or one that best describes how you feel about your neighborhood.

My neighborhood is _____ .

Answer the following questions about your topic sentence.

1. Is it a complete sentence?

2. Does it express an opinion?

3. Is it too general?

4. Is it too specific?

5. Does it have a controlling idea?

6. Can it be supported by examples?

TASK 6 The following are three possible topic sentences; add items from the list in task 1 above that can be used as supporting ideas to those below each topic sentence. You may use other items you can think of to support a topic sentence.

Topic sentence: My neighborhood is convenient.

Supporting ideas: Post office

Shopping center

_____

_____

_____

_____

_____

_____

_____

Topic sentence: My neighborhood is quiet.

Supporting ideas: People in the neighborhood are elderly retirees.

It is away from traffic.

_____

_____

_____

_____

_____

_____

_____

_____

Topic sentence: I like my neighborhood.

Supporting ideas: It is safe.

It is convenient.

_____

_____

_____

_____

_____

_____

_____

_____

Example   39

Activity 1.8

Writing a Rough Draft

TASK 1 Use your topic sentence in task 5 of Activity 1.7 and relevant supporting ideas to write a rough draft.

_____

_____

_____

_____

_____

_____

_____

_____

_____

_____

_____

_____

_____

_____

_____

_____

TASK 2 Use the following questions to edit your paragraph.

1. Does your paragraph have a topic sentence?
2. Does the topic sentence have a controlling idea?
3. Does your paragraph have enough support sentences?
4. Are all the support sentences relevant? Do they support the controlling idea?
5. Are the support sentences ordered from the weakest to the strongest?
6. Does your paragraph have a conclusion?
7. What kind of conclusion is it?

PART IV: ENABLING GRAMMAR EXERCISES

Structure and Use of the Simple Present Tense

The topic sentence and support sentences in an example paragraph are usually in the simple present tense. A topic sentence expresses an opinion, and the present tense is used to state an opinion. In addition, some support sentences are facts, which are stated in the simple present tense.

Basic Sentence Structure—Simple Present Tense

The simple present tense of the verb –be comes in three different forms: **am** (for first person singular), **is** (for third person singular), and **are** (for all other subject pronouns).

Basic Sentence Structure	Examples
Subject + verb (be) + complement	I am tired. He is tired. She is tired. We are tired. You are tired. They are tired.

Use the base form of verbs other than the verb -be for the simple present tense except when a third person singular is the subject of the sentence, in which case an -s is added to the verb as shown below.

Basic Sentence Structure	Examples
Subject + verb (any verb other than –be) + (complement) Subject + verb + s (any verb except –be) + (complement)	I drink coffee. You drink coffee. We drink coffee. They drink coffee. He drinks coffee. She drinks coffee.

Use of Simple Present Tense

Habitual statements, factual statements, statements that express an opinion, information about self or another person, definitions, and giving directions are all in the simple present tense. Below are examples of these types of sentences in the simple present.

1. The sun rises in the morning and sets in the evening. (Factual statement)

2. Washington D.C. is the capital of the U.S. (Factual statement)

3. I take a shower every day. (Habitual activity)

4. I go out to dinner once a week. (Habitual activity)

5. I think it is going to rain. (Opinion)

Example   41

6. I have brown eyes. (Information about self)

7. Chopsticks are two pieces of sticks used to pick up food to eat. (Definition)

8. Go straight and turn left. (Giving directions)

Opinions

Opinions, often in the simple present tense, can be used as a topic sentence as well as support sentences in example paragraphs.

Example

He strikes me as an honest person.

el me parece

Exercise 1.1

Opinions

TASK   Use each of the items below to write a sentence that expresses an opinion about your neighborhood.

Example:	(believe)	**I believe my neighborhood was established in 1897.**
1.	(believe)	I believe my neighborhood was established in 1985.
2.	(think)	I think my neighborhood has very good location.
3.	(seem)	My neighborhood seems clean.
4.	(feel)	I feel my neighborhood is a very safe place.
5.	(appears)	Many younger people appear everywhere in my neighborhood
6.	(looks)	My neighborhood looks like a nice place

7. (in my opinion) *In my opinion, my neighborhood has cultural diversity.*

8. (the way I see it) *The way I see it is a convinence place to start to live as an independent person.*

9. (strikes me as) *My neighborhood strikes me as a family area.*

Factual Statements

Factual statements are used as support sentences in paragraphs; they can be very convincing. It is important, therefore, to be able to write as well as recognize facts. We can distinguish a fact from an opinion, or better yet, a lie because a fact can be proven. We can measure it, observe it, or look it up. The simple present tense is often used to state a fact.

Examples

The sun sets in the evening.

Washington D.C. is the capital of the U.S.

The two statements above are facts. For the first example, all one has to do is walk outside and see the sun set. As for the second example, we can look it up in reliable sources.

Exercise 1.2

Factual Statements

TASK Write factual statements about your country of origin. The statements you write may be about the following:

1. Capital *Bogota is the capital of colombia*

2. Population *The population in Bogotá is about 10 million people.*

3. Life expectancy *The life expectancy of a dog is 15 years!*

4. Independence or national day *The Independence or national day of colombia on July 20.*

5. Climate *The climate in Bogotá is around 60°.*

6. National pastime *People from Bogotá like to visit Boyaca as National pastime*

Example   43

7. Colors of the national flag _The colors of the national flag of Color_

8. Staple food _The staple food in Colombia is "Bandeja   are 4, B, R_
   are   bes
   Paixe"

9. Language spoken by the majority of people in the country _is Spanish_

10. The system of government _is democratic_

11. Size of the country _is 45 million people_

12. Seasons _are summer and winter._

Habitual Activities

The simple present is also used for writing statements about habitual activities, or things done on a regular basis. One way to show regularity is the use of adverbs of frequency. Frequency adverbs can be divided into two types: positive and negative as shown below.

FREQUENCY ADVERB			
Positive	**Example**	**Negative**	**Example**
Always	I always come to class.	Never	He never comes to class.
Almost always	I am almost always present.	Almost never	I am almost never absent.
Usually	I usually go to the movies.	Seldom	I seldom go to the movies.
Often	He often takes the bus.	Rarely	I rarely eat lunch at school.
Sometimes	I sometimes study in the library.	Hardly ever	She is hardly ever on time.
Occasionally	I occasionally go jogging.		

Use of Frequency Adverbs

Place the frequency adverb after the verb, "be." With any other verb, the frequency adverb comes before. However, in verb phrases with one or more auxiliaries, the frequency adverb is placed after the first auxiliary. Note the position of the frequency adverb in relation to the verb or verb phrase in the examples below.

Examples

He is **always** late.

She **always** comes to class.

I have **always** been a good student.

Exercise 1.3

Use of Frequency Adverbs

TASK   Write sentences with the appropriate frequency adverb from the table above to show how often the following occur in your neighborhood. Pay attention to the positioning of the adverb of frequency.

Example: **Streetlights:**   **The streetlights in our neighborhood seldom go out.**

1.   Trash collection: Usually the trash collection are Monday, Wednesday and Fryday.

2.   Garage sales: Almost always garage sales old furniture.

3.   Crime: The crime is always punished with jail.

4.   Accidents: Almost always the accidents hurt people.

5.   Neighborhood picnics or parties: The neighborhood picnics always are at th park.

6.   Lights go out: The porches almost always have lights go out dering the day.

7.   People move in or move out: Often people move out in summer season.

8.   Snow removal: Always the snow removal is early morning.

Example   **45**

Personal Information about Self or Others

Personal information such as the kind on an identification card can be used as factual statements to support an opinion. For example, if you believe somebody is good looking, you have to describe physical characteristics to support your opinion.

Exercise 1.4

Personal Information about Self or Others

TASK   Use the given ideas to write complete sentences about yourself.

1. Given name: _____
2. Family name: _____
3. Hair color: _____
4. Color of eyes: _____
5. Height: _____
6. Weight: _____
7. Nationality: _____
8. Marital status: _____
9. Native language: _____
10. Street you live on: _____

Exercise 1.5

TASK   Use the given information and a verb in the simple present tense to form sentences.

1. Kim / brown eyes

   _____

2. Van / Vietnamese

   _____

3. Xiao / black hair

   _____

4. Jose / slim

_____

5. Susan / single

_____

6. Momodou / curly hair

_____

7. Patel / married

_____

8. She / a student

_____

9. James / short, curly hair

_____

10. Mustafa / a teenager

_____

DETERMINERS

Singular count nouns need a determiner to indicate specificity, generality, quantity, etc. Determiners are also used with plural nouns and non-count nouns for the same purpose.

ARTICLES

A set of determiners that are commonly used in English are articles: **a**, **an**, and **the**.

Examples		*Meaning*
1.	Umbrellas are useful in Seattle. (No article)	Umbrellas in general
2.	**An** umbrella can come in handy in Seattle.	Any umbrella
3.	**The** umbrella you gave me for Christmas came in handy in Seattle.	Specific umbrella
4.	**A** computer is a necessity in college these days.	Any computer
5.	Computers are necessary in college these days. (No article)	Computers in general
6.	**The** computer my parents bought me runs well.	A specific computer

Example   **47**

Exercise 1.6

Determiners

TASK   Fill in the blanks with the appropriate article and make changes in capitalization where necessary. Put an O in the blank if an article is not necessary.

1. _Ø_ Homework can be time consuming.

2. _The_ Homework our ESL teacher gave us took me five hours to complete. *[margin: Specific]*

3. _The_ Questions on our last quiz were difficult. *[margin: plural specific]*

4. _A_ Writing assignment can be rewritten. *[margin: General Singular]*

5. _Ø_ Final writing exams are not usually rewritten.

6. _The_ Topic for the final essay was confusing. *[margin: Specific]*

7. _A_ Topic is a subject to write about.

8. _An_ Apple a day keeps the doctor away.

9. _Ø_ Homework doesn't have to be done at home. *[margin: General]*

10. _An_ Assignment can be done either in class or at home. *[margin: General]*

11. _An_ Athlete can be a role model. *[margin: General]*

12. _A_ Professional athlete has long been considered a role model. *[margin: General]*

13. _Ø_ Professional athletes make a lot of money these days. *[margin: plural]*

14. _A_ Pop quiz is a short test that usually takes five to ten minutes. *[margin: General]*

15. _Ø_ Quizzes are important; students must take them seriously. *[margin: plural Gene]*

16. _The_ African elephant is in danger of becoming extinct.

17. _Ø_ African elephants are in danger of becoming extinct.

18. _Ø_ Man is in danger if he doesn't take care of his environment. *[margin: All people]*

19. _Ø_ Tigers are found in Asia. *[margin: plural General]*

20. _Ø_ Women athletes deserve equal opportunity. *[margin: plural]*

Other determiners that indicate quantity are used with count and non-count nouns. It is important to know whether a noun is count or non-count for proper use of quantifiers.

Exercise 1.7

TASK Indicate whether the noun is count or non-count by putting C for count or N for non-count on the line next to the noun.

1. _C_ Table
2. _C_ Chair
3. _N_ Furniture
4. _C_ Car
5. _N_ Traffic
6. _N_ Sugar
7. _N_ Milk
8. _N_ Wine
9. _N_ Transportation
10. _C_ Machine
11. _N_ Cheese
12. _N_ Homework
13 _N_ Work
14. _C_ Assignment
15. _N_ Statistics
16. _N_ Snow
17. _C_ Audience
18. _N_ Salt
19. _N_ Spice
20. _N_ Stuff

QUANTIFIERS

Count	Non-count	Both count and non-count
Few	Much	A lot
Many	Little	Some
A few — Some	A little	Lots
Several		

Example   49

Exercise 1.8

TASK   Put a check on the line next to the word or phrase that can be used in the place of the bold faced, underlined word in the sentence.

1. I need **<u>many</u>** eggs to bake the birthday cake.
    - ✓ a few
    - ✓ some
    - ∅ much
    - ∅ lots
    - ∅ little
    - ✓ a lot of

2. I spent **<u>many</u>** sleepless nights in this room.
    - ✓ few
    - ∅ much
    - ✓ some
    - ∅ too much
    - ✓ too many
    - ✓ quite a few

3. I put **<u>some</u>** cubes of sugar in my coffee.
    - ∅ few
    - ∅ much
    - ∅ a lot
    - ✓ lots of
    - ∅ little (quantity not size)
    - ✓ too few

4. He puts **<u>too much</u>** sugar in his coffee.
    - ✓ little
    - ∅ a lot
    - ✓ a lot of
    - ∅ lot of
    - ∅ many

5. **<u>Many</u>** cars were involved in the traffic accident.
    - ✓ a lot of
    - ✓ five
    - ___ lots
    - ✓ lots of
    - ___ a little
    - ✓ as many as twenty

6. That car uses **too much** gas.
   ✔ little
   _____ many
   ✔ a lot of
   ✔ many gallons of
   _____ few gallons
   ✔ lots of

7. I ate **too much** candy.
   _____ all
   ✔ some
   _____ almost all of *thu*
   _____ all of *the*
   ✔ many
   _____ little
   ✔ a lot of
   _____ lots

8. There were **many** people at the party.
   ✔ a lot of
   ✔ twenty
   ✔ a few
   _____ little
   ✔ very few
   ✔ lots of

9. I ate **some** of the fruit salad.
   _____ all of
   _____ much
   _____ some of
   _____ many
   ✔ all
   ✔ most

10. I have been there **a few** times.
    ✔ many
    ✔ several
    ✔ two
    _____ a little
    _____ too much
    ✔ too many

Example   51

Exercise 1.9

TASK   Find the mistakes and correct them.

1. Most of students in my class speak at least three languages.
2. Almost the students in my ESL 41 are bilingual.
3. Very a few students were absent yesterday.
4. Allmost all the students in my class turned in their assignment.
5. Most the students come to class on time.
6. There was too many traffic on the beltway this morning.
7. Many of students who came to the picnic yesterday had a green shirt on.
8. Most of people who saw the movie liked it.
9. I have a final for almost all of classes I am taking this semester.
10. Most of teachers were at the picnic.

Handwritten annotations:
- Top right: Add "the" for specific situation / In General NO "the"
- 1. *the* (inserted before students)
- 2. *all of* (above "the")
- 4. *Almost of*
- 5. Most of the students → specific
- 6. *much* (above "many")
- 7. *the* (inserted)
- 8. *the* ; Specific situation ; Most people who (General)
- 9. *the* (inserted)
- 10. *the* (inserted) ; Specific situation

UNIT TWO
Process

PART I: THE PROCESS PARAGRAPH

Processes occur every day in our lives. As a matter of fact, our daily routines are processes. For instance, on a weekday, we may wake up, get up, take a shower, get dressed, eat breakfast, go to work or school, etc. In other words, from the time we start the day, we are involved in a series of activities that are timely ordered. In addition, instructions on how to install a computer are in the form of a process. That is, we start from the first step and continue methodically until we put all the pieces together to make it work.

In some processes, steps occur in a given time order. Other processes, however, are methodical steps taken to cover a space. For example, when describing the tour of a building, we often begin from the main entrance and make our way to the other rooms in some kind of order determined by the tour guide. A piece of writing with this type of development is organized spatially. We begin from one location and proceed to the next and so on until the entire building is covered.

In this unit, you will study how to write process paragraphs. You will work on writing a chronologically developed paragraph and a spatially ordered paragraph.

Activity 2.1

Paragraph Analysis

TASK   Read the following paragraphs and answer the questions that follow.

Paragraph A

When I was growing up, the only body piercing I saw were the earlobes of women; however, nowadays, not only do I see men's earlobes pierced with jewelry hanging down one or both ears, but I also see piercing of various parts of the body of men and women ranging from the head, to the chest to the abdomen. First of all, I have seen pierced eyebrows with jewelry hanging over the eyelid. The right eyebrow, the left eyebrow, or both are pierced, and the usual piece of jewelry for this part of the body is a ring as opposed to a stud. Moving down from the eyebrow are pierced nostrils. Again, one or both nostrils are pierced and the jewelry of choice is usually a stud. However, I have also seen rings dangling over nostrils or from the ligament between the nostrils. Moving yet another step down is the upper lip; here piercing can occur anywhere from left to right. To my surprise and sometimes horror, is the piercing of the tongue. Although it is mostly out of sight, I have seen studs posted on the tongue when the person laughs or begins to talk. Next is the lower lip. Similar to the upper lip, it may also be pierced at different locations. Further down the body are the nipples of young muscular men. Here, the jewelry of choice is a ring. Lastly are pierced bellybuttons, or anywhere within the vicinity of the navel. Body piercing is so common that I am no longer surprised by the sight of any jewelry dangling from any part of the body of a man or woman.

Paragraph B

In order to be a student in the English as a Second Language (ESL) program at Northern Virginia Community College, one has to complete the application process, take the placement test, and register for the class in which he or she is placed. To begin with, the prospective student has to apply to the college by filling out an application form. This form can be obtained online or from the college. Subsequent to applying to the college, the applicant takes the placement test, the results of which are available soon after taking the test; however, the applicant may be required to do a writing sample before being placed at a level. Finally, the student can register by phone, online, or in person and pay the tuition. As you can see, it is really easy to enroll in the ESL program of Northern Virginia Community College.

1. Is paragraph A ordered chronologically or spatially?
2. Is paragraph B ordered chronologically or spatially?
3. Does paragraph A have a topic sentence?
4. Does paragraph B have a topic sentence?
5. In what order are the steps in paragraph A presented?
6. In what order are the steps in paragraph B presented?
7. Does paragraph A have a concluding sentence?
8. Does paragraph B have a concluding sentence?
9. What kind of conclusion is used in paragraph A?
10. What kind of conclusion is used in paragraph B?

PART II: ELEMENTS OF A PROCESS PARAGRAPH

Activity 2.2

The Topic Sentence of a Process Paragraph

The topic sentence of a process paragraph may be a statement that gives your opinion about the procedure. For example, one may have the opinion that it is easy to enroll in the ESL program at Northern Virginia Community College; thus the topic sentence of a paragraph that discusses the process would be, "It is easy to enroll in the ESL program at Northern Virginia Community College." Of course such a topic sentence will be followed by the steps to show why the writer believes it is easy to enroll in the program.

The topic sentence of a process paragraph may also state categories or steps in the process. For instance, a topic sentence about enrolling in the ESL program at NVCC may be as follows: "In order to be a registered student in the English as a Second Language program at Northern Virginia Community College, one has to complete the application process, take the placement test, and pay the tuition." This topic sentence states categories, but the paragraph has to give the specific steps taken to register.

Similarly, a topic sentence on body piercing can also be as follows: "Body piercing can be seen on the head, chest, and abdomen of young men and women." In this case, the main idea of the paragraph puts the usually pierced parts of the body into three categories: those on the head, the chest, and the abdomen. This spatially ordered paragraph will begin from the head and proceed down to the abdomen. Topic sentences of process paragraphs can be developed by chronologically or spatially ordering specific steps in the process.

TASK   The type of process, i.e., chronological or spatial may also be stated explicitly or it can be inferred. Read the following topic sentences and for each, decide whether it is for a chronologically or spatially ordered paragraph. Also identify the word or phrase that states or suggests the type of process, chronology or space.

Example

Astronauts can locate continents and some specific landmarks on earth as they rotate around the globe.

Type of process: _Spatial_____

Process marker: _Locate, landmarks_____

1.   There is more to buying a house than finding the one you like, moving in, and paying the mortgage.

Type of process:_____

Word or phrase that suggests type of order: _____

2. The contiguous 48 states of the U.S. have four time zones: Eastern, Central, Mountain, and Pacific.

   Type of process:_____

   Word or phrase that suggests type of process: _____

3. There are four basic steps to becoming a licensed driver: studying for the written test, taking the written test, learning to drive, and taking the road test.

   Type of process:_____

   Word or phrase that suggests type of process: _____

4. Registering for this class is a multi-step process.

   Type of process:_____

   Word or phrase that suggests type of process: _____

5. Doctors take a number of steps to diagnose a disease.

   Type of process:_____

   Word or phrase that suggests type of process: _____

6. Members of a soccer team are assigned to specific areas of a soccer field.

   Type of process:_____

   Word or phrase that suggests type of process: _____

7. There is a procedure you must follow in order to withdraw from this class.

   Type of process:_____

   Word or phrase that suggests type of process: _____

8. He has tattoos all over his body.

   Type of process:_____

   Word or phrase that suggests type of process: _____

Activity 2.3

Support Sentences

The support sentences of a process paragraph are the steps to reach the goal, objective, result, or destination. The steps are ordered with the help of connectors. There are three basic types of connectors: those that suggest initial step, those that refer to second and/or subsequent steps, and those that are used to signal final step.

Connectors used to signal initial step

First

Firstly

First of all

To begin with

Connectors used with second and/or subsequent steps

Second

Secondly

Next

Moving on / down

Subsequent to

Subsequently

After that

Afterwards

Another

Yet another

Then

Connectors used to signal final step

Finally

Lastly

Last of all

In the end

TASK   Read the two sample paragraphs above, underline the connectors, and list them in the designated columns that follow.

Connectors used in the body piercing paragraph

_____

_____

_____

_____

_____

_____

_____

Connectors used in the paragraph on becoming a student at Northern Virginia Community College

_____

_____

_____

_____

_____

_____

_____

Activity 2.4

The Concluding Sentence

The concluding sentence of a process paragraph can be a restatement. This is sometimes the case especially for paragraphs with a topic sentence that states an opinion about the process. For example, a paragraph with a topic sentence that expresses the ease of registering for a language program may have the concluding sentence: "As you can see, it is not difficult to enroll in this program." Such a concluding sentence is reiterating the opinion expressed at the beginning given the steps outlined in the paragraph. Likewise, a topic sentence such as: "the bedrooms in my apartment have been strategically located," can be restated as "The bedrooms in my apartment have been located in such a way that I can have natural light, see sunrises and sunsets, and enjoy the ocean view."

Another type of concluding sentence is one that states the result of the process. This is particularly applicable to the chronologically ordered paragraph. What the concluding sentence is saying is that if you go through these steps, this will be the result. An example of this type of conclusion is as follows: "If you successfully complete these steps, you will realize the American dream: owning your own house." A statement of result can also be used as the concluding sentence of a spatially ordered paragraph. After all, if you follow the steps going from one location to the next, you will have covered the entire premises, the result of the process.

Yet another type of concluding sentence is a comment. Having stated a goal or an objective and showing the steps taken to achieve it, you can make a concluding remark about the process. It is important to note, though, that the comment has to be in reference to the process and result discussed in the paragraph. In paragraph B above, for example, the writer's concluding sentence is the comment that he is no longer surprised when he sees jewelry on various parts of the body of a man or woman.

TASK   Write a possible concluding sentence for each of the topic sentences in the task of activity 2. You may use a restatement, result, or a comment as your concluding sentence. The first one has been done for you.

1. There is more to buying a house than finding the one you like, moving in, and paying the mortgage.

   If you successfully complete these steps, you will realize the American dream: owning your own house. ____

   _____

   _____

   _____

2. The contiguous 48 states of the U.S. have four time zones: Eastern, Central, Mountain, and Pacific.

   _____

   _____

   _____

3. There are four basic steps to becoming a licensed driver: studying for the written test, taking the written test, learning to drive, and taking the road test.

    _____

    _____

    _____

    _____

4. Registering for this class is a multi-step process.

    _____

    _____

    _____

    _____

5. Doctors take a number of steps to diagnose a disease.

    _____

    _____

    _____

    _____

6. Members of a soccer team are assigned to specific areas of a soccer field.

    _____

    _____

    _____

    _____

7. There is a procedure you must follow in order to withdraw from this class.

    _____

    _____

    _____

    _____

8. He has tattoos all over his body.

    _____

    _____

    _____

    _____

PART III: WRITING YOUR PROCESS PARAGRAPH

Activity 2.5

Differentiating Between Chronologically Ordered and Spatially Ordered Paragraphs

Whether you choose to develop a paragraph spatially or chronologically may depend on what you want your readers to know. For example, if you decide to write a paragraph about the layout of your house including the number of floors, different rooms and their locations in relation to other rooms, you are writing a spatially ordered paragraph. On the other hand, if you choose to write about the building of the house starting from obtaining a building permit, to planning, construction, doing the electric work, furnishing, and finally moving in, you are writing a chronologically ordered piece.

TASK   For each of the following topics, decide whether you would develop a paragraph on it chronologically or spatially. Give a few initial steps in the process to show how you would most likely develop such a paragraph.

Example

Buying a car

__X__ Chronologically

_____ Spatially

First, study consumer reports. Next, narrow down your choices. Visit dealerships. Then apply for a loan.

1. Writing a paragraph

   _____ Chronologically

   _____ Spatially

   Steps in the process: _____

   _____

   _____

2. Your last trip

   _____ Chronologically

   _____ Spatially

   Steps in the process: _____

   _____

   _____

3. The seating on an airplane

_____ Chronologically

_____ Spatially

Steps in the process: _____

_____

_____

4. How you registered for your class

_____ Chronologically

_____ Spatially

Steps in the process: _____

_____

_____

5. Getting married

_____ Chronologically

_____ Spatially

Steps in the process: _____

_____

_____

6. Renting an apartment

_____ Chronologically

_____ Spatially

Steps in the process: _____

_____

_____

7. Becoming a licensed driver

_____ Chronologically

_____ Spatially

Steps in the process: _____

_____

_____

8. The seating at a family dining table

  ____ Chronologically

  ____ Spatially

  Steps in the process: _____

  _____

  _____

9. Giving someone a tour of your house or apartment

  ____ Chronologically

  ____ Spatially

  Steps in the process: _____

  _____

  _____

10. Making your favorite dish

  ____ Chronologically

  ____ Spatially

  Steps in the process: _____

  _____

  _____

Activity 2.6

Getting Ideas for Chronologically Ordered Paragraphs

TASK   To write a chronologically ordered paragraph, you must have the steps you go through to reach a certain goal. Think, for example, of all the things you do on a typical workday before leaving for school or work and jot them down. Do not pay too much attention to order and spelling at this point.

My morning routine: Things I do every morning before I leave for work.

Wake up

Get up

_____

_____

_____

_____

_____

_____

_____

_____

Below are steps in an individual's morning routine.

Wake up

Take a shower

Brush my teeth

Get up

Get dressed

Read the paper

Make breakfast

Iron my clothes

Do the dishes

Check the oil

Leave for work

Start the car

Turn the alarm off

ORDERING STEPS

TASK   When writing a chronologically ordered process paragraph, it is important that you put your steps in order of time. The activities in the morning routine above are not in chronological order. Number the items so that they are in time order. Compare your numbered list to that of the other students. Are there differences? Some differences in order may be based on habit. Do the same with your own list.

Activity 2.7

Categorizing Steps in a Process

TASK 1   Below is a list of steps one has to take to become a student at Northern Virginia Community College. Some of them are about the application process. Can you think of other categories?

Step 1:   Apply for admission and financial aid
Step 2:   Obtain an NVCC catalog
Step 3:   Take placement tests
Step 4:   See a counselor
Step 5:   Register for classes
Step 6:   Pay your tuition
Step 7:   Access your free student e-mail account
Step 8:   Check your registration schedule
Step 9:   Buy a parking permit
Step 10:   Buy your books

A.   Application process

B: _____

C: _____

D: _____

E: _____

Activity 2.8

Getting Ideas for Spatially Ordered Paragraphs

Unlike the chronologically organized process paragraph, the spatially ordered paragraph focuses on ground covered step by step going from one location to the next. Instead of going from time to time, we go from space to space. In either case, the steps occur in a certain order.

TASK 1 The following is a list of body piercing as seen on the physical structure of young men and women. Can you add other pierced parts of the body you have seen?

Earlobes

Eye brows

Nostrils

Bellybutton

Ligament dividing nostrils

Upper lip

Chest

Tongue

Lower lip

Chin

_____

_____

_____

_____

SPATIAL ORDERING

TASK 2 Rearrange the pierced parts of the body in a clear order, unidirectional or otherwise.

Categorizing Pierced Parts by Location

TASK 3 Think of possible groupings of the pierced parts above.

(a) Those on the head _____

(b) _____

(c) _____

TASK 4 Complete the following outline with information from paragraph A on body piercing.

Topic Sentence:

    I.   Head
           Earlobes
           Eyebrows

           _____
           _____
           _____
           _____
           _____
           _____

    II.   Chest

           _____
           _____

    III. Abdomen

           _____
           _____

TASK 5 Think of the steps you would take to show someone your school. Where would you begin? What buildings or rooms would you visit and in what order?

_____

_____

_____

_____

_____

_____

_____

_____

_____

_____

_____

Writing Assignment

1. Write a paragraph in which you discuss the process of getting married in your country of origin.

2. Write a paragraph in which you discuss the process of renting a house or an apartment. Make sure that you include all the steps, and put them in order.

PART IV: ENABLING GRAMMAR EXERCISES

Prepositions

Group A

The prepositions **in, on,** and **at** are among the most commonly used. Below are uses of these prepositions in relation to time and place.

	Time		Place
In	Century	(In the 21st century)	World (In the world)
	Year	(In 2003)	County (In Arlington County)
	Month	(In July)	Country (In the United States)
	Season	(In the summer)	Province (In the province of . . .)
			School, (class/library/cafeteria)
On	Date	(On July 4th)	Street (On Pennsylvania Avenue)
	Day	(On Monday)	Floor (On the second floor)
	Weekday	(On weekdays)	Field (On the soccer field)
	Weekend	(On weekends)	Campus (On campus)
At	Specific time	(At 5:00 P.M.)	Address (At 1600 Penn. Avenue)
	Noon	(At noon)	Domicile (At his house)
	Midnight	(At midnight)	Place of work (At my office)
	Sunset	(At sunset)	School (At school)
	Night	(At night)	Location (At the bottom/top/end)
	Sunrise	(At sunrise)	
	Bedtime	(At bedtime)	

Exercise 2.1

TASK   Fill in the blanks with the appropriate one of the three prepositions: **in, on,** and **at.**

1. Two weeks from now, I will be lying _____*at*_____ the beach in the Bahamas.
2. He got to my house _____*at*_____ midnight.
3. Stop calling me _____*at*_____ my bedtime.
4. I came to the U.S. _____*in*_____ 1995.
5. I live _____*on*_____ the second floor of that building.
6. I don't believe that we are now _____*in*_____ the 21st century.
7. She likes to go to the movies _____*on*_____ weekends.
8. Topic sentences are usually _____*on*_____ the top of a paragraph.
9. Thesis statements are usually _____*in*_____ the bottom of an introductory paragraph.
10. He asked me to meet him _____*at*_____ his house.

11. I was living ____at____ Patrick Henry Drive when you came to visit me last year.
12. Independence Day is ____on____ July 4th.
13. He has the habit of having a snack ____at____ midnight.
14. Polluters must realize that we are ____on____ this world together.
15. I do not watch TV ____on____ weekdays.
16. My family lives ____in____ The Gambia, West Africa.
17. I spent my holiday ____at____ the province of Quebec ____in____ Canada.
18. He lost his ring ____on____ football field.
19. I was living ____On____ campus when I was an undergraduate student.
20. Students who attend a community college usually live ____at____ home.

Group B

Other prepositions are used in reference to the location of objects, people, and places, etc. in relation to other objects, people, places, etc.

Prepositions	Examples
Across from	The car is parked across from the library.
Next to	He was sitting next to me in class yesterday.
In front of	My car skidded and hit the car in front of me.
Before	He was standing before me in the checkout line.
Beside	He was sitting beside her.
On the left/right	The living room is on the left.
Between	The library is between the bank and the courthouse.
Above	His apartment is above mine.
Below	His office is directly below mine.
Over	The chandelier is hanging over the dining table.
Beneath	The shovel is beneath that pile of snow.

Group C

Prepositions are used with verbs to form idioms or fixed expressions. As fixed expressions, the meanings and structures of these phrases do not change. For example, the phrasal verb "to look over" means "to review." These idioms are commonly used by native speakers when speaking and writing. I am sure you have heard many of them or have come across some of them in your readings. The verbs "**look**" and "**run**" are often used with prepositions to form idioms. See the examples below.

Look up	I look up new words in the dictionary.
Look over	I always look over my assignment before I hand it in.
Look into	I am looking into buying a new car.
Look down on	He looks down on me.
Look out	He told me to look out for speeding cars.
Look up to	I look up to my older brother.
Look after	I look after her child when she is at work.
Run out	I seldom run out of gas.
Run over	"Are you trying to run me over?" complained the pedestrian.
Run into	I run into him at the mall every weekend.

Exercise 2.2

TASK Think of prepositions used with the following verbs to form idioms. Try to come up with as many as you can and discuss them as a class. Also, make sure that you know the meaning of each of the idioms you come up with.

Come

Put

Call

Stand

Hand

Fill

Turn

Exercise 2.3

TASK Fill in the blanks with the appropriate idiom. In some cases, a noun or pronoun may come between the verb and the preposition that form the idiom.

1. Even though he makes many careless mistakes, he never ___look over___ his work before he __turns__ it __in__.
2. Here is my telephone number. ___Call___ me ___back___ if you have any questions.
3. I ___ran out___ of money, so I had to return home even though I was enjoying my vacation.
4. Can you ___put off___ the meeting until next week? I will be out of town this week.
5. I ___ran into___ my teacher in my neighborhood. I had no idea we lived in the same neighborhood.
6. If you happen to be in my neck of the woods, please ___come over___.
7. We have to ___call off___ the wedding. The bride changed her mind about getting married.
8. He ___stands out___. He doesn't look like anyone in the group.

Ordinals

The ordinals listed below are used either as pronouns or adjectives. When used as adjectives, they modify the noun that comes right after. However, as pronouns they take the role of a noun including subject, object, object of a preposition, etc.

Another
Other
Others
The other
The others

A sentence may have the pronoun ***another, others, the other,*** or ***the others*** as its subject. ***The other*** and ***the others*** as the subject of a sentence, suggest that they are the remaining items. The following ordinals: ***Other, another,*** **and** ***the other*** are also used as adjectives to modify a noun.

Examples

The following sentences show ordinals as pronouns, adjectives, and as indicators of remaining items.

Ordinals as Pronouns

He has many kids in college. One is a junior; *another* is a senior.
I have two brothers. One goes to NVCC, and *the other* goes to GMU.
Some students transfer to George Mason University; *others* transfer to Virginia Tech.
Some students come to class on time, and *the others* always come late.

Ordinals as Adjectives

One student is talking, *another* student is laughing, and *the other* students are quiet.
Some students come late; *other* students come early.
Five students came to class. Two came on time, and *the other* students came late.

Ordinals That Signify the Number of Items That Remain

We have two new students; one is from China, and *the other* is from Egypt.
I have three five-dollar bills. One is in my left pocket; *the others* are in my hand.

Exercise 2.4

TASK Carefully study the sentences above and complete the grid below. For each of the ordinals, check the appropriate box to indicate whether it is a singular or plural pronoun or an adjective that modifies a singular or plural noun. Also check the appropriate box to indicate whether or not the ordinal signifies the number that remains. The first one has been done for you.

	As pronoun		As an adjective that modifies		Signifies remaining item(s)	
	Singular	Plural	Singular noun	Plural noun	Singular	Plural
Another	X	–	X	–	–	–
Other						
Others						
The other						
The others						

Exercise 2.5

TASK Read the following sentences carefully and determine whether the ordinal in each sentence is a pronoun or an adjective. If the ordinal is a pronoun, put "**Pron.**" in the space provided, and if it is an adjective, put "**Adj.**" in the space.

1. There are two students from Bolivia in this class. One is male, and **the other** is female. _P_

2. Ten students went on the fieldtrip. Five took the Metro, and the **other** students drove. _Adj_

3. I have two roommates. One is moving out today, and **the other** is moving out next week. _P_

4. Three students were absent. One was sick, **another** went back to his country, and **the other's** car broke down. _P_ _Adj_

5. My parents will not come to visit because one does not like to fly, and **the other** can't stand the cold weather. _P_

6. There are three main steps to becoming a student in this program. One is to apply for admission, **another** step is to take a placement test, and **the other** is to pay the tuition. _Adj_ _P_

7. I have five siblings. One is in elementary school; two are in high school, and **the others** are in college. ___P___

8. Whenever I buy a pair of shoes, the left shoe always fits like a glove, but **the other** shoe is always tight. ___Adj___

Exercise 2.6

TASK   Fill in the blanks with *another, other, others, the other,* or *the others.*

1. He has five tattoos. One is on his right arm, __another__ is on his left arm, and __the other__ tattoos are on his back.

2. There are four basic steps to becoming a licensed driver. The first step is to study for the written test, __another__ is to take the written test, and __the other__ steps are to learn how to drive and to take the road test.

3. The contiguous 48 states of the U.S. have four time zones. One is Eastern, __another__ is Central, yet __another__ is Mountain and __the other__ time zone is Pacific.

4. The writing process includes four important steps. The first step is to generate ideas, and __another__ step is to do an outline. One __other__ step is to write a rough draft. Finally, you must edit your rough draft.

5. I can't believe how much I was able to accomplish today. First, I did my food shopping for the week. __Another__ thing I did was change the oil in my car, which I had been putting off for weeks. __The other__ things I accomplished were balancing my checkbook, paying the rent, and writing and mailing dozens of Christmas cards.

6. I have three assignments. I will do one today and __the other__ two tomorrow.

7. He owns two cars. One is an American car, and __the other__ is a Japanese car.

8. We have two bathrooms. One is on the first floor, and __the other__ is on the second floor.

9. We have three bedrooms. One is in the basement, __Another__ is on the first floor, and __the other__ is on the third floor.

10. We have three telephones. One is on the first floor, and __the other__ are on the second floor.

UNIT THREE
Description

OBJECTIVES

By the end of this unit, you should be able:

- ◼ to use sensory details in description

- ◼ to construct the topic sentence of a descriptive paragraph

- ◼ to state parts of an object, their relationship to other parts, and their function or use

- ◼ to distinguish between action and non-action verbs and use noun clauses

- ◼ to compose and edit a rough draft of a descriptive paragraph

---

PART I: THE DESCRIPTIVE PARAGRAPH

In describing a person, place, activity, or object, you are helping the reader form a picture of what you have seen or experienced. To help the reader get a clear picture, you may focus on tangible characteristics. Those characteristics may include ones that can be seen, heard, smelled, tasted, or felt. In other words, the five senses can be used in describing a person, place, activity, or object.

In addition, you may include information that is not discernable by using the five senses. Such information includes the function of the object or activity, traditions associated with it, personal experience, etc. Descriptive paragraphs focus on the characteristics or features that help readers realize what the object, place, or person is like. Unlike definition, which tells us what the subject is, description tells us what the subject is like.

In this unit, you will work on writing descriptive paragraphs.

Activity 3.1

Paragraph Analysis

TASK   Read the following paragraph and answer the questions that follow.

Our Fish Pond

We have a fishpond in our backyard. It is kidney shaped and is about eight feet long, four feet wide, and eighteen inches deep. It has a thick plastic lining which covers the inside and up to 6″ over the edge. The piece of plastic that is over the edge of the pond is covered with tightly wedged in flagstones which form a flat surface and a line that gives the pond its distinct kidney shape. The pond holds about 250 gallons of water. In the pond, there are four water lilies that bloom in midsummer. When in bloom, they have pink and blue flowers that open up every day between midmorning and late afternoon. The pond also has fish, which like to swim as a school in the afternoon when the sun is directly overhead. They like to chase each other, and every now and then, one jumps up and plops back into the pond. There is also a frog that lives in the pond, but it likes to sit on the flagstones on the edge of the pond. The slightest noise will make it jump back in. The pond is in the middle of a triangular shaped bed that has three varieties of Japanese maples, one in each corner. Also in this bed are different plants including a white butterfly bush, echinacea, a dwarf Japanese pine, elephant ears, a small-leaf rose bush with mini white flowers, and various types of ground cover. The pond, as the main feature in the garden, is there for aesthetic purposes. It also has therapeutic effect, for it is a good place to wind down after work. As one sits there and watches the fish, butterflies, the occasional hummingbird, and water lilies and smells the fragrance from the flowers around the pond, one tends to calm down.

1. Does the writer use sensory detail in the paragraph?
2. Which of the senses are used?
3. Would you say the description is vivid?
4. Does the description include function or use?

PART II: ELEMENTS OF A DESCRIPTIVE PARAGRAPH

Activity 3.2

The Topic Sentence of a Descriptive Paragraph

Similar to a topic sentence of an example paragraph, the topic sentence of a descriptive paragraph can be an opinion. Some opinions may be supported by actions while others can be supported by description. For instance, if I am of the opinion that the view outside my window is beautiful, I may have to describe the view in such a way that someone who has not seen it would agree with me. Such a description would have to be vivid; it may include colors, shapes, sizes, shades, etc.

Similar to other topic sentences, the topic sentence of a descriptive paragraph includes a topic and a controlling idea. The topic is what is going to be described, and the controlling idea is an opinion expressed that has to be supported by description, characteristics, or features that exemplify the idea expressed about the person, place, or object.

TASK   Read the following topic sentences and underline the controlling ideas. Under each topic sentence, list the type of characteristics or features you would expect in the body of a paragraph that supports it.

1. There is a spectacular view from my balcony.
    Characteristics or features: _____

    _____

    _____

    _____

2. She dressed up for her daughter's wedding.
    Characteristics or features: _____

    _____

    _____

    _____

3. The party was a disaster.
    Characteristics or features: _____

    _____

    _____

    _____

4. He has a gorgeous house.
   Characteristics or features: _____

   _____

   _____

   _____

5. The crowd was unruly.
   Characteristics or features: _____

   _____

   _____

   _____

6. He has lost a lot of weight.
   Characteristics or features: _____

   _____

   _____

   _____

7. I have a comfortable car.
   Characteristics or features: _____

   _____

   _____

   _____

8. She is wearing a colorful dress.
   Characteristics or features: _____

   _____

   _____

   _____

9. We had a rowdy class yesterday.
   Characteristics or features: _____

   _____

   _____

10. The beach was crowded.
    Characteristics or features: _____

    _____

    _____

Activity 3.3

Support Sentences

The support sentences of your descriptive paragraph basically depict the scenery, object, or the situation you have in mind and the opinion you put forth in your topic sentence. You should take for granted that the readers of your paragraph have not seen what you are describing; as a result, you make them see, hear, feel, or when necessary, even know what the item tastes like.

What support sentences you use in a descriptive paragraph, therefore, depends on the topic and the controlling idea expressed in the topic sentence. For instance, there are many characteristics that can be used to describe a person, but in your descriptive paragraph, you have to choose a set of characteristics that helps you portray the character or picture you wish to illustrate. If you say that someone is beautiful, for example, you have to come up with the physical features that support your assertion. However, if you want to prove that someone is a good leader, you might concentrate on personality.

Unlike describing a person, when describing an object, you may include different parts of the object and their functions. Secondly, you might describe in detail your perception of each of these smaller units. Let us say that you wish to write a paragraph in which you describe desks found in college classrooms. Your first step is to list the parts of a desk and then provide the color, shape, size, relationship, and use of each of the parts of a desk.

When you describe a scenery or view, however, you are expected to show the features of the landscape, objects, and colors. If you have the opinion that the view from your window is beautiful, the description of the scenery has to include features that you think would be pleasing to the eyes of your audience.

TASK   Describe in detail the characteristics or features listed under one of the topic sentences in the task of activity 3.2 above. Make sure that your descriptions are vivid. In other words, try to use colors, shapes, texture, smell, sound, etc., to help you make what you are describing seem real.

Activity 3.4

The Concluding Sentence

The concluding sentence of a descriptive paragraph can be a restatement of the topic sentence. If the main idea, i.e., the topic sentence expresses an opinion you have about an object, for example, your concluding sentence might reiterate that opinion after having supported it with characteristics and features in the body of your paragraph.

A comment is another type of conclusion you may choose to use in a descriptive paragraph. Let us say that you are looking for an apartment to rent, and you go with a real-estate agent to see a number of apartments. It turns out that you saw one that you really liked. On your return, you tell a friend that you saw your dream apartment, and then you go on to describe the unit. In the end, you may say, "This is the best apartment I have ever seen." This concluding statement indicates how you feel about the apartment after asserting that it is your dream apartment and characterizing its distinctive features.

Yet another concluding sentence can be a statement that summarizes the features and characteristics in the body of your descriptive paragraph combined with a comment or restatement of the topic sentence.

PART III: WRITING YOUR DESCRIPTIVE PARAGRAPH

Activity 3.5

Generating Ideas

Below are ideas and concepts based on the five senses, experience, or background knowledge that can be used in describing a person, object, scene, or activity. Each part of an object can be described in terms of its color, shape, size, texture, smell, taste, or how it feels. Its background, function, or use can also be part of the description. Familiarize yourself with the words and their meanings.

FIVE SENSES						WHAT YOU KNOW
Sight		**Hearing**	**Smell**	**Taste**	**Feeling**	**Experience/Knowledge**
Color	*Texture*	*Noise*	Sweet	Sweet	Rough	History
Red	Rough	Loud	Foul	Sour	Smooth	How it works
Blue	Smooth	Shrill	Pungent	Tangy	Rugged	Where it is found
Green	Rugged	Low		Salty	Coarse	Origin
Black	*Length*			Bitter		Traditional use if any
White	Long					Function / use
Gray	Short					What happened?
Shape	Medium					Where did it happen?
Round	Extra long					When did it happen?
Oval	*Depth*					Consequences
Square	Deep					
Rectangular	Shallow					
Pentagon	*Width*					
Octagon	Wide					
Nonagon	Narrow					
Hexagon	Tight					
Size	Loose					
Small	*Physical*					
Large	Thin					
Medium	Slim					
Petite	Fat					
Miniscule	Heavy					
Minute	Overweight					
Extra large	Chubby					
	Short					
	Tall					

A: Describing a Person

When describing a person, one way to generate ideas is to list the characteristics the individual has. You can then choose those that best meet your needs in supporting the main idea of your paragraph.

TASK 1   List the characteristics you would associate with the following people.

1. A model
    Characteristics: _____
    _____
    _____
    _____

2. A hyperactive child
    Characteristics: _____
    _____
    _____
    _____

3. A handsome man
    Characteristics: _____
    _____
    _____
    _____

4. A football player
    Characteristics: _____
    _____
    _____
    _____

5. A beautiful woman
    Characteristics: _____
    _____
    _____
    _____

6. A homely person
   Characteristics: _____

   _____

   _____

   _____

7. A good teacher
   Characteristics: _____

   _____

   _____

   _____

8. A depressed person
   Characteristics: _____

   _____

   _____

   _____

9. A homeless person
   Characteristics: _____

   _____

   _____

   _____

10. An unhappy child
    Characteristics: _____

    _____

    _____

    _____

B: Describing an Object

TASK 2 Below is a list of the parts of a desk. Carefully study the desk you are sitting on or any desk and fill in the blanks in the table below.

Part	color	material/texture	size/shape	relation to other parts	use
Seat	yellow	vinyl/smooth	large/square	attached to frame	to sit on
Back rest	_____	_____	_____	_____	_____
Frame	_____	_____	_____	_____	_____
Book rack	_____	_____	_____	_____	_____
Arm rest	_____	_____	_____	_____	_____

TASK 3 Write complete sentences that describe your desk by giving the color, texture, size, the function of each part and the relationship between parts.

Example

The arm rest / color

The arm rest is yellow.

1. The seat / size

   _____

2. The frame / material

   _____

3. The book rack / in relation to seat

   _____

4. The arm rest / use

   _____

5. Back rest / shape

   _____

6. The seat / in relation to the frame

   _____

7. Book rack / function

   _____

8. Arm rest / color

   _____

9. Frame / function

   _____

10. Back rest / function

    _____

C: Describing a Scenery or View

When you describe a scenery or view, you are expected to show the features of the landscape, objects, and colors. If your opinion is that the view from your window is beautiful, the description of the scenery has to include features that show beauty.

TASK 4 List the features you associate with the following places or sceneries.

1. A golf course
   Features: _____
   _____
   _____
   _____

2. A beautiful sunset
   Features: _____
   _____
   _____
   _____

3. A desert
   Features: _____
   _____
   _____
   _____

4. A jungle
   Features: _____
   _____
   _____
   _____

5. A graveyard
   Features: _____
   _____
   _____
   _____

6. The view from somewhere in your house or apartment
   Features: _____

   _____

   _____

   _____

7. A skyline
   Features: _____

   _____

   _____

   _____

8. A picket line
   Features: _____

   _____

   _____

   _____

9. A schoolyard
   Features: _____

   _____

   _____

   _____

10. The beach
    Features: _____

    _____

    _____

    _____

TASK 5   Below are ideas, places or things that were mentioned by international students in describing their first impressions of the U.S. Would you say some of these were part of your first impressions? Have you had similar first impressions in another city or country? If so, add them to the list.

Diversity
Sizes of people
Roads
Cars
Traffic
Houses
Lawns

Greenery
Cleanliness
Language
Food

_____
_____
_____
_____
_____
_____
_____
_____
_____
_____
_____

Activity 3.6

Sensory Details

Sensory details, things you can see, hear, taste, smell, or feel, are used in describing people, places, or objects. Such details make descriptions vivid. For example, the extent to which the U.S. is diverse can be realized based on the colors of people, their physical features, and languages or accents heard. Some sense perceptions, however, are not applicable in some situations.

TASK 1 Add sensory and other details to those below each of the topics

1. Diversity
    Colors
    Physical features
    Dress
    Language

_____
_____
_____
_____

2. Sizes of people
   Height
   Sizes of clothing

   _____

   _____

   _____

   _____

3. Roads
   Width
   Number of lanes

   _____

   _____

   _____

   _____

4. Cars
   Makes
   Colors
   Sizes

   _____

   _____

   _____

   _____

5. Traffic
   Number of cars
   Speeds with which cars are moving
   Traffic lights

   _____

   _____

   _____

6. Houses
   Colors
   Types of houses
   Sizes
   Material

   _____

   _____

   _____

7. Lawns
   Size
   Color of grass
   Texture

   _____

   _____

   _____

   _____

8. Greenery
   Trees
   Lawns
   Shrubs

   _____

   _____

   _____

   _____

9. Language
   Accent
   Slang
   Formal / informal

   _____

   _____

   _____

   _____

10. Interaction between people
    Lively
    Distance

    _____

    _____

    _____

11. Snow
    Color
    Texture

    _____

    _____

    _____

TASK 2 Describing what one did, how it was done, how he or she felt, and what was used, can help some-one who wasn't present to get a clear picture of what happened. In the following exercise, try to be more descriptive in such a way that one could get a clear picture of the activity, event, place, or person you are describing. Try to make your description as vivid as possible.

1. My first day at this school

   _____

   _____

   _____

   _____

2. What I had for breakfast / lunch / dinner

   _____

   _____

   _____

   _____

3. My teacher

   _____

   _____

   _____

   _____

4. Your neighborhood late at night

   _____

   _____

   _____

   _____

5. Your favorite dish

   _____

   _____

   _____

   _____

6. A friend or relative

_____

_____

_____

_____

7. Your house or apartment

_____

_____

_____

_____

8. Public buses in the U.S.

_____

_____

_____

_____

9. Your favorite dress or clothes

_____

_____

_____

_____

Writing Assignment

1. Write a paragraph in which you describe your school or campus. Include as much detail as possible. Also remember to use sensory detail so that one could form a picture of what the school or campus is like.

2. Write a paragraph in which you describe a friend or a relative. Use vivid description to help a reader form a picture of the person you are describing.

3. Describe what you went through to take classes at this school. Describe what you did, and how you felt.

4. Describe an object from your country. Include what you know about this object, your experience with it, and sensory details.

PART IV: ENABLING GRAMMAR EXERCISES

Action / Non-action Verbs

Verbs that express the five senses, opinion, possession and feeling do not occur in the progressive tense when used to express involuntary action. However, similar verbs may be used to express voluntary action, in which case it can occur in the progressive.

Example

The food tastes good.	(Verb expresses the sense of taste.)
She is tasting the food.	(Verb expresses the action of tasting. The person is actually putting the food on her tongue to see what it tastes like.)

Exercise 3.1

Determine which of the following sentences is correct, and if a sentence is not correct, give reasons why it is wrong.

1. He is tasting the food.   *he tastes the food*
2. The food is tasting good.   *C*
3. The chef is tasting the soup.   *The chef tastes the soup*
4. Are you hearing me?   *C*
5. I am listening to the news.   *I listen to the news*
6. I am seeing the sunset.   *I see the sunset*
7. He is seeing her.   *He see her*
8. I am feeling good.   *I feel good*
9. I am feeling my way around the city.   *I feel my way around the city.*
10. She is smelling the food.   *She smells the food.*
11. It is smelling good.   *C*
12. He is feeling the heat from the sun.   *He feels the heat from the sun.*
13. The perfume is smelling good.   *C*
14. He is smelling the deodorant.   *He smells the deodorant*
15. She is tasting the drink.   *She tastes the drink.*

Verbs that express opinion, possession, and feeling do not occur in the progressive.

Example

I think it is going to rain. (Verb expresses speaker's opinion about whether it is going to rain or not.)

I am thinking about my assignment. (Verb expresses the action of using the brain; the speaker usually shows signs of looking inside himself or herself—eyes half closed, head tilted, chin in hand, etc.)

I have a car. (Possession)

The class is having a picnic. (Students are at the park eating, playing games, and enjoying themselves.)

I love my wife. (Verb expresses feeling for one's wife.)

Exercise 3.2

Use each of the following non-action verbs to write a sentence that expresses an opinion, possession, or feeling.

1. Believe

   I believe in my organizational skills to develop projects.

2. Think

   I think that complete the studies in the university is the best option to get a better job.

3. Have

   I have three beautiful daughters. Two of them are twins and the other one is a baby.

4. Know

   I know how to cook turkey for thansgiving dinner.

5. See

   I see my daughter playing in the park.

6. Hope

I hope you are doing very well.

7. Love

I love my husband.

8. Hate

I hate messy rooms.

9. Detest

I really detest bad behaviors.

10. Abhor

I abhor the abortion.

Noun Clauses

The structure of a noun clause depends on whether the clause was formed from a statement, yes/no question, or information question. To form a noun clause with a statement, put the relative pronoun **that** in the initial position followed by the statement as shown below.

Statement: He had been a good student.

Noun clause: **That he had been a good student** surprised me.

Statement: He is always late.

Noun clause: **That he is always late** doesn't surprise me.

Statement: She speaks fluent English.

Noun clause: I know **that he speaks fluent English.**

To form a noun clause with a yes/no question, begin the noun clause with "whether" or "if" followed by the subject, the verb or verb phrase, and the complement, in that order.

Yes/no question: Did he do his homework?

Noun clause: **Whether he did his homework** is not my concern.

Yes/no question: Has he gone home?

Noun clause: I don't know **if he has gone home.**

Yes/no question: Has he been watching television all day?

Noun clause: I really don't know **whether he has been watching television all day.**

To form a noun clause with information questions, begin with the WH-question word followed by the subject, and put the verb or verb phrase in final position.

WH-question: Where has he been?

Noun clause: I have no idea **where he has been.**

WH-question: Whose car is that?

Noun clause: I don't know **whose car that is.**

WH-question: When was he here?

Noun clause: I have no idea **when he was here.**

Note: If the WH-question includes an object or place, the object or place comes after the WH-question word and is followed by the subject and verb or verb phrase.

WH-question: What book had he been reading?

Noun clause: I didn't know **what book he had been reading.**

WH-question: What city is he from?

Noun clause: I don't know **what city he is from.**

Exercise 3.3

Change each of the following sentences into a <u>noun clause in the past perfect or <u>past perfect progressive</u></u> tense so that the noun clause can be the object of a sentence that begins with "I didn't know..."

Example

Where was he?

I didn't know where he had been.

1. Did he leave?

   I didn't know if he had leaved.

2. Where did he go?

   I didn't know where he had gone.

3. Who went with him?

   I didn't know who has been gone with him.

4. How many of them were in the car?

   I didn't know how many of them have been in the car.

5. What city was their destination?

   I didn't know what city has been their destination

6. When did they leave?

   I didn't know when they have leaved.

7. He drove too fast.

   I didn't know that he has driven too fast.

8. He got a speeding ticket.

   I didn't know that he has gotten a speeding ticket.

9. What kind of car was he driving?

   I didn't know what kind of car he has been driving.

10. Did Mike go with them?

    I didn't know if Mike has gone with them.

11. How long were they gone?

    I didn't know how long they have been going.

12. Where else did they go?

    I didn't know where else they have gone.

13. Were they glad to be back?

I didn't know if they have been glad to be back.

14. They were away for three weeks.

I didn't know that they have been away for three weeks

15. What city did they plan to visit next?

I didn't know what city they have planned to visit next.

Exercise 3.4

Rewrite the following pairs of sentences so that the first action in the past perfect or past perfect progressive is the subject, object or objective of a preposition, and the verb and complement give the second action in the simple past.

Example

He had a fever. This worried me.

That he had had a fever worried me.

1. My parents were surprised. I was studying diligently.

   _____

2. I failed. This surprised my parents.

   _____

3. Something shocked my friends. I wanted to drive home drunk.

   _____

4. What did he do? This was the talk of the town.

   _____

5. Where was he? This was the mystery.

   _____

6. Did he exceed the number of absences allowed? That was what he wanted to know.

   _____

7. I was interested in something. Where was he all the time?

   _____

8. Something worried me. He went for days without eating.

   _____

9. I was a student of his. He didn't know this.

   _____

10. Something was amazing. He was a student for seven years before he graduated.

   _____

UNIT FOUR
Narration

OBJECTIVES

By the end of this unit, you should be able:

- ▪ to state distinctive features of a narrative

- ▪ to determine the point of view from which a narrative is written

- ▪ to identify main characters in a narrative

- ▪ to state the climax and describe the denouement

- ▪ to compose and edit a rough draft of a narrative

PART I: THE NARRATIVE PARAGRAPH

A narrative is a story. We all have stories to tell; be they personal narratives, fairy tales, stories with legendary characters narrated for children, or fables, which are stories with animal characters that are told to teach children a moral—what is right or wrong. Fairy tales and fables in a given culture are passed on from generation to generation. For example, Cinderella is a fairy tale often narrated in western culture. Many traditions have a version of the Cinderella story. What is your culture's version of this famous story? Can you remember other stories you were told as a child?

A personal narrative is one's life history. For example, you may have been born and brought up in a particular region in your country of origin and later in life moved to another region or a different country. The events that lead to such a move are often compelling stories. Other kinds of stories you have probably recounted are personal experiences. For instance, if you went on vacation, you may tell stories about places you visited, people you met, and experiences you had on the trip.

A narrative includes characters, setting (or place where the actions occurred), events that lead to a conflict or climax, and a resolution of the conflict. However, some stories may not include a resolution of the conflict; instead, it is left to the reader to figure it out.

You may write a narrative from one of two points of view: first or third person. If you are one of the characters in a story you are telling, you may recount the story in the first person. However, if you are not one of the people in the story, you tell it in the third person.

In this unit, you will learn to write a narrative in which you tell a personal experience you have had or an incident you have witnessed.

Activity 4.1

Paragraph Analysis

Following is an incident that occurred in a classroom. Read the narrative and answer the questions that follow.

An Encounter between Two Immigrant Students of Different Generations

One of my ESL students, who had tattoos, body piercing, and was dressed in baggy pants, a T-shirt, and cap with the visor turned backwards, was sitting at the second desk from the front on the far left row. While I was teaching, he got up and left the room. Minutes later, he returned with a small bag of snacks that he had apparently bought from the vending machine down the hall. He sat back at his desk and tried to open the bag, but it made a lot of noise, which got the attention of the students who looked at him with disgust. He realized that he was drawing attention; as a result, he put the bag back on his desk. He didn't give up though; he waited for an opportune moment, such as when there was laughter, to try again to open the bag, but it still made noticeable noise. In an attempt to give it one more try, the bag crackled, at which time another student, old enough to be his mother, who was sitting in front of him, turned around, grabbed the bag, and placed it on her desk. The student looked stunned. "That's a good idea," said one student. Many of the other students nodded in agreement. The lady defiantly kept the bag on her desk until the class ended; then she gave it back to him.

1. Where did the story take place?
2. Who is telling the story?
3. What point of view is used in the story?
4. Who is the main character?
5. Who are the other characters?
6. Are the events in the narrative spatially or chronologically ordered?
7. What would you say is the climax?
8. What is the resolution of the conflict?

PART II: ELEMENTS OF A NARRATIVE PARAGRAPH

Activity 4.2

The Topic Sentence

Stories are told for different reasons. Fables and fairy tales, for example, can be used to teach children a lesson. For example, in West African storytelling tradition, after recounting a fable or fairy tale, children are told the moral or point of the story and what lessons to learn from the narrative or from individual characters. Animal characters in African fables have distinct characteristics. For instance, the rabbit is wise and cunning, the hyena is greedy, the leopard is the gentleman of the forest, and the lion is the king of the forest, etc.

Fables and fairy tales have fixed expressions as openings such as "once upon a time." Personal stories, on the other hand, can begin with a statement that indicates the point of the story. For example, a young man can begin or end a narrative by saying, "I should have listened to my mother's advice." Such a statement of regret, if used as the main idea of the paragraph, is followed by the series of events that lead to the lesson learned.

Other stories are told to make a point. The title of the narrative in Activity 4.1—"An Encounter between Two Immigrant Students of Different Generations"—suggests a point the writer has in mind, which is that people of different generations behave differently. A reader could come to the same conclusion even if the narrative did not have that title.

Storytellers may begin with a motivator or an invitation to listen. A common motivator is "guess what happened." At that point, the listener replies with the question "what?" The teller then narrates the story.

You should not begin a paragraph in academic writing with an invitation to listen. The best topic sentence for a narrative is a statement that indicates the lesson learned or point of the narrative. As in paragraphs of other rhetorical modes, the topic sentence can be at the beginning of the paragraph or implied.

TASK   Read each statement carefully and decide whether or not it is a good topic sentence for a narrative paragraph. Also suggest series of events you think can follow such a statement.

1. That was my lucky day.
2. Today might as well be Friday the 13th.
3. You won't believe all the things that happened to me today.
4. You know what . . .
5. I learned my lesson.
6. I should have listened to my parents.

Activity 4.3

The Support of a Narrative Paragraph

The body of a narrative paragraph is comprised of the series of events that make up the story. Similar to the chronologically ordered process paragraph, in which the steps occur in time order, the events in a narrative must appear in the order they happened.

Other information in the body paragraph may include descriptions of the setting, characters, and props. For example, in the previous sample narrative, the writer describes the main character, the younger student, to show how people of his generation dress in contrast to older students of a different generation.

TASK 1 Below are the events in the narrative above; however, they are not in chronological order. Number the events so that they are time ordered. The first event has been done for you.

a. _____ Laughter
b. _____ Another attempt to open the bag of snacks
c. ____1____ Class in progress
d. _____ The class ends
e. _____ Student walks out to get a snack
f. _____ Other students show disguist
g. _____ Older student returns bag of snacks to owner
h. _____ Student returns to classroom with snack
i. _____ A third try to open the bag
j. _____ Student tries to open the bag of snacks
k. _____ Older student grabs bag

TASK 2 Sentence and other connectors are used to help a writer show the order in which the events occur in a story. Identify the time connectors used in the narrative in Activity 4.1, and state the period it indicates in the stream of events. The first two are done for you.

1. While: co-occurrence (i.e., leaving the classroom while the class is in progress)
2. Minutes later: when student returned to classroom
3. _____
4. _____
5. _____
6. _____

TASK 3 Body paragraphs may include descriptions of characters, setting, and props. Descriptions make stories engaging. The five senses (smell, taste, feeling, sight, and hearing) are used in descriptions. Reread the story and determine the events in which each of the senses is used.

1. Smell:

2. Taste:

3. Feeling:

4. Sight:

5. Hearing:

The writer of a narrative recounts the story in the first person or third person depending on whether or not the author is one of the characters. In either case, the exact words of a character can be used in the story, or the writer may choose to use indirect speech. It is important to know the mechanics of writing direct speech and indirect speech. See the enabling grammar exercises at the end of this unit.

Activity 4.4

The Concluding Sentence

Some stories end with a phrase that states just that: "The End." Fairy tales and fables may have a fixed expression that ends the narrative. For instance, "They lived happily ever after" may be used to conclude a fairy tale. Personal stories, however, teach us a lesson or a moral; as a result, a narrator may state the lesson learned as the conclusion. In fact, in a narrative paragraph, a topic sentence, which expresses the idea the story exemplifies may be restated as the concluding sentence. The writer of the sample narrative could have used the statement "Something happened that made me believe that mothers know best" as the topic sentence and then told the story to illustrate his belief, because the character in the narrative that came up with the solution to the problem was a mother. The statement "As you can see, mothers know best" can be a concluding sentence. In this case, the writer sees the story as an example of the adage, "Mothers know best." Can you think of other possible concluding sentences for the narrative? Share your suggestions with a partner or the class as a whole.

Proverbs and Sayings as Lessons or Morals

TASK   Stories are told to make a point, teach a lesson, or reiterate a moral. Such consequences are stated as truisms, sayings, proverbs, or aphorisms. Which of the following statements can be used as a result of the narration in Activity 1? Can you think of others?

1. Mothers know best.
2. Never behave in a way that makes you stand out.
3. Action is louder than voice.

4. _____
5. _____
6. _____

PART III: WRITING YOUR NARRATIVE PARAGRAPH

Activity 4.5

Getting Ideas

TASK   Try to remember an event, and jot down ideas to complete the following outline. The event may be a cultural misunderstanding you had, your first day in a different city or country, or an incident you witnessed. At this point, do not include details.

Setting: Where did the event take place?

Characters: Who are the people in the story?

Events: List the series of events you can remember. The numbers below are simply suggestions; your story may have more than five main events or fewer than that.

1.

2.

3.

4.

5.

Climax: The most exciting point in the series of events

Resolution: How was the problem solved?

Activity 4.6

Writing a Rough Draft

TASK   From the outline of your story in Activity 4.5, write a rough draft of the narrative. Make sure that you include the main events and that they are in chronological order.

Activity 4.7

Editing

TASK   Read your paragraph as many times as the number of mistakes you usually make. In other words, if you are one who makes spelling, pronoun reference, and subject-verb agreement mistakes, you need to read your paragraph three times concentrating on one problem area at a time.

PART IV: ENABLING GRAMMAR EXERCISES

Direct Speech and Reported Speech

Direct speech and reported speech are commonly used when telling a story. It is important to know the mechanics involved in using direct and indirect speech in your paragraph.

Exercise 4.1

Study the sentences that follow and notice the use of quotation marks and other punctuation in direct speech.

1. He said, "I will register for ESL 31."

2. She said, "What classes are you taking this semester?"

3. She says, "I have registered for ESL 31 and ESL 32."

4. "I am tired. I want to go home," he said.

5. "I am sleepy," he said. "I want to go to bed."

6. She said, "When is the assignment due?"

7. "When is the assignment due?" she said.

8. He said, "Is the assignment due today?"

9. The teacher said, "Hand in your assignment on time."

10. She said, "Do not look at other students' work during the test."

11. I asked him if he would go to the library with me and he said "Sure."

12. "Watch out!" she said. "There is a pothole."

As shown in the sentences provided, the speaker's exact words are in quotation marks. Periods, question marks, and exclamation marks are inside the quotation marks, not outside the quotation, a common mistake in writing direct speech.

Exercise 4.2

Punctuate the following sentences and use capital letters when necessary.

1. She said I turned in my assignment yesterday
2. It was due yesterday he said you must be kidding me
3. Do you know the professor's e-mail address he said
4. It is on the syllabus she said
5. I can't find my syllabus he said I misplaced it
6. The teacher said do not talk in any language during the test
7. He said be quiet during the test
8. When do we have our next test asked one student
9. He says I like grammar
10. The teacher says I expect you to turn in your assignments on time
11. I am sorry I cannot go to the movies with you I have to study she said I have an exam tomorrow morning
12. Good morning he said it is a pleasure to meet you

When writing a story, you may choose to use reported speech as opposed to direct speech. For instance, the exact words by one of the students,

"That is a good idea,"

could have been reported as

One student said that it was a good idea.

In this case, the tense is changed from present to past because the verb that comes right before the exact words of the speaker in quotation is in the past tense. When this verb is in the past tense, change the tenses as follows:

Present is changed to past

He said, "I am tired."

He said that he was tired.

Past is changed to past perfect

He said, "I was at home."

He said that he had been at home.

Past perfect does not change

He said, "I had been there many times."

He said that he had been there many times.

Other changes are made depending on the type of sentence used in the direct speech in quotation marks as follows.

Statement

To change a statement into reported speech, add the relative pronoun "that" to the statement preceeded by the subject and the introductory verb.

Example

He said, "I did my homework."

He said that he had done his homework.

Information Question

The sentence word order changes in reported speech. The subject of the sentence in direct speech is placed right after the question word in the reported speech and is then followed by the verb or verb phrase.

Example

"What did he do?" he asked.

He asked what he had done.

Yes/No Question

When changing a yes/no question into reported speech, place "if" or "whether" after the introductory verb followed by the subject, verb, or verb phrase and the rest of the sentence.

Example

"Did he go home?" he asked.

He asked if he had gone home.

Command

To change a command into reported speech, place "to" after the object pronoun, which is then followed by the base form of the verb and the action demanded.

Example

He said, "Be quiet."

He told me to be quiet.

Command with the Negative Marker "Not"

To change a command with the negative marker "not," place "not to" after the object pronoun, which is then followed by the base form of the verb and the action demanded.

Example

He said, "Do not talk."

He told me not to talk.

Exercise 4.3

Change the following into reported speech and change the verb to the appropriate tense as necessary.

1. He said, "I will register for ESL 31."

   _____

   _____

2. She said, "What classes are you taking this semester?"

   _____

   _____

3. She says, "I have registered for ESL 31 and ESL 32."

   _____

   _____

4. "I am tired. I want to go home," he said.

   _____

   _____

5. "I am sleepy," he said. "I want to go to bed."

   _____

   _____

6. She said, "When is the assignment due?"

   _____

   _____

7. "When is the assignment due?" she said.

   _____

   _____

8. He said, "Is the assignment due today?"

   _____

   _____

9. The teacher said, "Hand in your assignment on time."

   _____

   _____

10. She said, "Do not look at other students' work during the test."

    _____

    _____

11. I asked him if he would go to the library with me and he said "Sure."

    _____

    _____

12. "Watch out!" she said. "There is a pothole."

    _____

    _____

13. "Will you come to my birthday party?" he asked.

    _____

    _____

14. He said, "I will be there."

    _____

    _____

15. "I will be a little late," he said. "I have to take my mother to the airport."

    _____

    _____

UNIT FIVE
Extended Definition

OBJECTIVES

By the end of this unit, you should be able:

- to determine the class of items with which you are familiar

- to construct hyphenated noun phrases

- to determine and state distinguishing characteristics using adjectives, adjective clauses, and hyphenated noun phrases

- to construct single sentence definitions including class and distinguishing characteristics

- to compose and edit a rough draft of an extended definition

---

PART I: EXTENDED DEFINITION

We often look up the definition of a word in a dictionary, but sometimes, we need more information than what a dictionary provides to fully understand the word in question. Helping an audience know the meaning of a word in a foreign language may be even more challenging. To explain the meaning of such a word, it may be necessary to use an extended definition that includes not only what the term being defined is, but what it is not.

Speakers of other languages often have to define ideas, objects, titles, phenomena, and the like when writing about a subject matter that is foreign to their native English speaking audience. Students who write about their cultures usually have to write extended definitions to help the teacher understand the topic about which they are writing. Therefore, it is important for non-native English speakers to know how to write extended definition as a system of development.

In this unit, you will work on writing an extended definition.

Activity 5.1

Paragraph Analysis

TASK: Read the following paragraphs and answer the questions that follow.

Daughter Rice Wine

Daughter Rice Wine is an alcoholic beverage that is made from rice. The wine comes from the Zhejiang Province of China. There is a beautiful story behind this important, traditional alcoholic beverage. As the story goes, a long time ago, when a baby daughter was born in this region in China, the parents would decorate a jar by carving or painting flowers on it. Then they would fill the jar with rice wine and bury it in the ground. When the daughter got married, the parents would dig out the rice wine and share it with the guests. As a result of this ancient tradition, we call the wine Nu En Hong Rice Wine, or Daughter Rice wine.

W. Wang

1. Does the definition include a class or category?
2. Does the definition contrast the subject with other members of its class?
3. Does the definition show what the subject is not?
4. Are there distinguishing characteristics that set the subject apart from other members of its class?

Birthday cake

A birthday cake is a baked food product that comes in different colors and flavors, but it is solely used in celebrating someone's birthday. The cake is usually decorated. In addition, the cake may have writing on it including the birthday person's name and the phrase: "Happy Birthday." A birthday cake may also have lighted candles. The number of candles may correspond to the person's age. For example, a five year old may have five candles on the cake. When the cake is brought out for the birthday person to see and appreciate, he or she often shows an element of surprise. According to tradition, those in attendance sing "happy birthday" to the person whose birthday they are celebrating. The birthday person does not usually sing along but waits for the song to end; at which time he or she makes a wish without telling the others and blows out the candles. The cake is then sliced into pieces and distributed to the people.

5. Does the definition include a class or category?
6. Does the definition contrast the subject with other members of its class?
7. Does the definition show what the subject is not?
8. Are there distinguishing characteristics that set the subject apart from other members of its class?

PART II: ELEMENTS OF AN EXTENDED DEFINITION

Activity 5.2

Single Sentence Definition as Topic Sentence

Unlike other expository paragraphs, an extended definition may not have a topic sentence that has a topic and a controlling idea. Because you are writing about what the term means as opposed to how you feel about it, an extended definition may not be a statement that expresses an idea or an opinion. The extended definition may begin with the topic, which is what is being defined, its class, and a distinguishing characteristic.

When you define a word, you are giving its meaning. In an extended definition, however, you are expected to give more details so that readers can fully understand the meaning of the concept, object, title, phenomenon, or whatever you are defining.

Definition Sentence

A definition sentence includes the object or idea being defined, a linking verb, class to which the item belongs, and distinguishing characteristic. The distinguishing characteristics can be a hyphenated noun phrase as in a "five-string instrument," adjectives, or adjective clause.

TASK   Read the definition sentences below and answer the questions that follow.

1. A community college **is a two-year post secondary institution.**
   a. What is the object or idea being defined?
   b. What is the linking verb?
   c. To what class does the item belong?
   d. What are the distinguishing characteristics?

2. A hanbok **is a long, colorful, Korean traditional** dress.
   a. What is the object or idea being defined?
   b. What is the linking verb?
   c. To what class does the item belong?
   d. What are the distinguishing characteristics?

3. A birthday cake **is** a baked food product **used in celebrating someone's birthday.**
   a. What is the object or idea being defined?
   b. What is the linking verb?
   c. To what class does the item belong?
   d. What are the distinguishing characteristics?

Activity 5.3

Hyphenated Noun Phrase

A hyphenated noun phrase is another element that can be used in a definition. Such a structure consists of a number, a hyphen, a noun in the singular form, a modifier, if any, and a noun or name of the item.

TASK 1 Change the following into hyphenated noun phrases.

Example

I bought a **compact car that has two doors.**

I bought a **two-door compact car.**

1. A college where it takes four years to get an undergraduate degree

   _____

2. One bill in the amount of hundred dollars

   _____

3. A young man that is twenty years old

   _____

4. A pole that is forty feet long

   _____

5. A general who has four stars

   _____

6. A building which has ten stories

   _____

7. A piece of pizza three days old

   _____

8. A report that is ten pages long

   _____

9. A process that has five steps

   _____

10. A visit that took three days

    _____

11. A stamp that costs thirty seven cents.

_____

12. A flight that took seven hours.

_____

TASK 2 Correct the mistakes in the following sentences with hyphenated noun phrases.

1. He gave me a five-dollars bill.

_____

2. I lost two ten-dollar bill.

_____

3. I saw five five-bedrooms apartment today.

_____

4. I live in ten-story building.

_____

5. I bought twenty one string instrument from him.

_____

6. He goes to a twoyear college.

_____

7. I just want to let you know that there is a two-hours wait.

_____

8. I took a five-week intensive English classes.

_____

9. He has a thirties-inch waist.

_____

10. I gave her a fifty-dollars gift certificate.

_____

Activity 5.4

Adjectives

You can use adjectives as distinguishing characteristics. Adjectives can help you define ideas, objects, titles, and phenomena. As modifiers, they help you state what something is or is not.

One or more adjectives can be used to modify a noun. However, if you use two or more adjectives, then you have to punctuate correctly. If, for some reason, you use two adjectives, place a comma between them; however, three or more adjectives are a series, so you should put a comma after each adjective and a connector before the last one.

Also make sure that the adjectives are in the correct order. The ordering of adjectives varies according to style. However, the general trend is to give the number of items, be evaluative, be descriptive, and state where it is from and what it is called. In other words, begin with a determiner followed by an adjective that expresses your opinion, then use adjectives that show what the item is like, including size, shape, texture, and color, and finally, give more specific information such as the origin and name of what it is you want to modify. As a rule, the multiple adjectives you use to modify a noun answer the following questions and are used in the same order.

1. How many?
2. What is your opinion about it?
3. What is it like? What size, shape, texture, or color is it?
4. Where is it from?
5. What is it?

A rule of thumb is to read out loud your series of adjectives and see how it sounds. If it doesn't sound good, it is probably not in the correct order. This is particularly helpful in determining the order of the adjectives that describe the object: size, shape, texture, and color. Keep rearranging them until the string of adjectives sounds good to you. Avoid using too many adjectives to modify a single noun at a time. Only use modifiers that are essential in defining the object.

TASK   For each of the following, write a sentence in which you use a linking verb and the given adjectives to modify the noun. Make sure that the adjectives are in the correct order.

Example

A station wagon / American / spacious / large / car

A station wagon is a spacious, large American car.

1. A cell phone / small / useful / device for speaking to others who are away from you

   _____

   _____

2. Disk / square / small / flat / utilitarian / black or silvery / device for storing information

   _____

   _____

3. Hanbok / long / colorful / beautiful / Korean / traditional / dress

   _____

   _____

4. A CD / round / modern / flat / device / for storing music or speech

   _____

   _____

5. Kora / twenty-one-string / musical / traditional / gorgeous / West African / instrument

   _____

   _____

6. Pinata / small / candy-filled / cute / paper / toy / for blindfolded kids to open by hitting it to get the candy

   _____

   _____

7. Chopsticks / round / smooth / light brown / two / ten-inch sticks for picking up food to eat

   _____

   _____

8. Jazz / American / beautiful / popular / music

   _____

   _____

Activity 5.5

Distinguishing Characteristics as Adjective Clauses

Some distinguishing characteristics appear in the form of an adjective clause, which either gives more information about a noun or helps the reader identify the noun it modifies.

Examples

The holiday **which falls on the fourth Thursday in November** is Thanksgiving.

Thanksgiving, **which falls on the fourth Thursday in November,** is a national holiday in the U.S.

In the first sentence, the adjective clause, "**which falls on the fourth Thursday in November,**" modifies the noun holiday; in addition, it helps us know that the holiday which falls on this day is Thanksgiving. In the second sentence, the same adjective clause modifies the noun, Thanksgiving; however, it simply gives more information about Thanksgiving. We do not need the adjective clause to know the holiday; we have the name. Because the clause is not necessary, it is separated from the main clause by commas. See the enabling grammar exercises at the end of this unit for more practice on adjective clauses.

TASK   Change the second sentence in each pair to an adjective clause that modifies the appropriate noun in the first sentence.

Example

American football is a contact sport.

It is different from soccer.

American football, which is different from soccer, is a contact sport.

   1. An e-mail is an electronic message.

       It is sent through the worldwide web.

       An e-mail, which is an electronic message, is sent through the worldwide web.

   2. Basketball is a game.

       In this game a player scores points by putting the ball through the opponents' basket.

       _____

       _____

3. The blues is said to have originated from West Africa.

    The blues is popular in the United States.

    The blues, which is popular in the USA, originated from West Africa.

4. Halloween is on October 31.

    On Halloween children go trick or treating.

    _____

    _____

5. Running a red light can be dangerous.

    It is a traffic violation.

    Running a red light, which is a traffic violation, can be dangerous.

6. A sophomore is a college student.

    This student is in his or her second year of college.

    A sophomore, who is a college student, is in his/her second year of college.

    A sophomore is a college student who is in her/his second year of college.

7. A Microwave is an appliance.

    Its functions include defrosting, heating, cooking, and making popcorn.

    A microwave is an appliance whose functions include defrosting, heating, cooking, and making popcorn.

8. Chopsticks are about ten inches long.

    They are used for eating.

    Chopsticks, which are about ten inches long, are used for eating.

PART III: WRITING YOUR EXTENDED DEFINITION

Activity 5.6

Generating Ideas

Determining Class of Subject

TASK In a definition, it is necessary to state the class to which the word being defined belongs. Work with other students or as a class to determine the class to which each of the following items belongs. Some of the items are from cultures foreign to the U.S. You may need the help of students from those countries (in parentheses next to those items.)

Subject	Class
Example: Community College	Post secondary institution or Institution of higher learning
Cellular phone	_____
	_____
Microwave	_____
	_____
CD	_____
A computer	_____
	_____
E-mail	_____
	_____
Basketball	_____
	_____
Groundhog Day	_____
	_____
Halloween	_____
	_____

A sophomore

_____

_____

Jazz

_____

_____

Running a red light

_____

_____

Fast food or junk food

_____

_____

Blind date

_____

_____

Prom

_____

_____

Tattoo

_____

_____

Body piecing

_____

_____

Piñata (Hispanic)

_____

_____

Dae bo reum (Korean)

_____

_____

Hanbok (Korean)

_____

_____

Fengshui (Chinese)

_____

_____

Aodai (Vietnamese)

_____

_____

Henna (Middle Eastern)

_____

_____

Qanun (Arabic)

_____

_____

Kora (West Africa)

_____

_____

Chopsticks (Oriental culture)

_____

_____

Steel drum (Caribbean)

_____

_____

Matreshka (Russia)

_____

_____

Activity 5.7

Listing Distinguishing Characteristics

TASK   Give the distinguishing characteristics of four ideas or objects. You may choose from the list above or use your own culture-specific subjects or ideas.

Example: **Subject**

Cellular phone:

Distinguishing characteristics

Cordless
Whole phone held in hand
Portable
Wireless
Mobility
Chimes, beeps, or vibrates instead of ringing

Subject   **Distinguishing characteristics**

(a) _____   _____

                                _____

                                _____

                                _____

                                _____

(b) _____   _____

                                _____

                                _____

                                _____

                                _____

(c) _____   _____

                                _____

                                _____

                                _____

                                _____

(d) _____   _____

                                _____

                                _____

                                _____

                                _____

Constructing One-sentence Definition

TASK Think of an idea or object from your culture that you want to define and try to come up with a one-sentence definition. Remember to include a category, class, and at least one characteristic to differentiate the word from other members of its class.

The following are examples:

Examples:

Subject: Praise-name   Ethnic origin: Traditional West African ethnic groups

A praise-name is a designation only used to speak highly of its bearer. _____

_____

_____

Subject: Xalam   Ethnic origin: Wolof, West Africa

Xalam is a Wolof five-string musical instrument. _____

_____

_____

(a) Subject:_____   Ethic origin: _____

_____

_____

_____

_____

_____

(b) Subject:_____   Ethic origin: _____

_____

_____

_____

_____

(c) Subject:_____   Ethic origin: _____

_____

_____

_____

_____

_____

Activity 5.8

Outline for the Extended Definition Paragraph

To write an extended definition, you have to have details including distinguishing characteristics other than the one in the initial definition sentence. A helpful step in the process of writing an extended definition of an object or idea is to do an outline that includes the class and its members, subcategory, and distinguishing characteristics. See example below:

Example

Topic: Birthday cake

Class: Baked food product

Members of the same class: Wedding cake

Cake for dessert

Cookies

Pie

Croissant

Subcategory: Cakes

Members of subcategory: Wedding cake

Cakes for dessert

Distinguishing characteristics: Decorated

Writing in frosting on cake

Candles

Ceremoniously brought out

Singing prior to eating the cake

Wish by birthday person before blowing out candles

Candles on cake blown out by birthday person

TASK Complete the following outlines with information on two topics of your choice, one from the U.S. and another from your country of origin. For each topic, make sure that you have the class, subcategory, and distinguishing characteristics.

Topic: _____ Language or ethnic origin: _____

Class:

Members of the same class:

Subcategory:

Members of subcategory:

Distinguishing characteristics:

Topic: _____ Language or ethnic origin: _____

Class:

Members of the same class:

Subcategory:

Members of subcategory:

Distinguishing characteristics:

Activity 5.9

Circular Definition

A common occurrence in students' extended definitions is circular definition, repeating the word being defined in giving its meaning. An example of circular definition is to say a birthday cake is a cake for a birthday. The definition simply repeats the name of the object being defined with a different word order. One way to avoid circular definition is to use the class and distinguishing characteristics instead of the name of the object being defined. For instance one can say that a birthday cake is a baked food product that is used to celebrate someone's birthday.

TASK   Correct the circular definition in each of the following sentences.

1. A cassette recorder is a recorder to play cassettes.

2. A cell phone is a phone for making and receiving phone calls.

3. A disc is a disc for storing data.

4. An e-mail is mail you can send or receive online.

5. A steel drum is a drum made of steel.

6. Chopsticks are sticks for eating.

7. A community college is a college for the community.

8. A TV is a television.

9. A bike is a bicycle for riding.

10. A snow shovel is a shovel for shoveling snow.

11. Directions are directions to someplace or for doing something.

12. A traffic light is a light for traffic.

13. A speeding ticket is a ticket for speeding.

14. A Christmas present is a present for Christmas.

15. A professional basketball player is a basketball player who plays professional basketball.

Activity 5.10

Writing a Rough Draft

TASK 1 Use the ideas in one of your outlines in activity 5.8 to write a rough draft. Make sure that you include as many ideas as you need to provide a clear definition of the term in question.

_____

_____

_____

_____

_____

_____

_____

_____

_____

_____

_____

_____

_____

_____

_____

_____

TASK 2 Use the following questions to edit your paragraph.

1. Does your definition include a class or category?
2. Does your definition contrast the subject with other members of its class?
3. Does the definition show what the subject is not?
4. Are there distinguishing characteristics that set the subject apart from other members of its class?

Writing Assignment

1. Write a paragraph in which you define a holiday in your country of origin. Remember to include the class or category to which the holiday belongs, other members of its class, and distinguishing characteristics that set the holiday from other members of its class.

2. Write an extended definition of a community college.

PART IV: ENABLING GRAMMAR EXERCISES

Adjective Clauses

A relative pronoun often begins an adjective clause, which is used to modify a noun. The adjective clause either simply gives more information about a noun, or it states a distinctive characteristic that helps to identify the noun it modifies.

Example

The student ***who is sitting by the door*** wants to leave early.

Tran Nguyen, ***who is sitting by the door,*** wants to leave early.

In the first example, the adjective clause—**who is sitting by the door**—modifies the noun, **student;** in addition, the clause helps the reader to know who wants to leave early. In the second example, the same adjective clause modifies the proper noun, **Tran Nguyen;** however, it simply gives us more information about Tran Nguyen. We don't need it to know who wants to leave early; we have her name.

Relative pronouns:

Pronoun	Used in relation to	Example
Who	person (Subject)	I saw the man who got the job.
Whom	person (Object)	Mary was the lady to whom I gave a ride.
Which	things	I returned the book which was overdue.
Whose	possession	The student whose car was totaled is absent today.
That	person and things	The paragraph that he wrote is interesting.
Where	place	He lives in an apartment where pets are not allowed.
When	time	He lived at a time when the cost of living was high.

Exercise 5.1

Underline the adjective clause in each of the following sentences and circle the noun each clause modifies.

1. The class that I want to take meets three times a week.

2. The teacher whose class I am taking is from Africa.

3. The used book which I bought from the book sale has the answers to all the exercises.

4. My friend who took this class last semester recommended it to me.

5. Early spring is the time when trees bloom.

6. The town where I was born is on the East Coast.

7. The person whom I look up to is my older brother.

8. Bring me the desk whose bookrack is broken.

9. The car that I bought uses a lot of gas.

10. The police officer who gave me a ticket was very polite.

11. The candidate whom I supported won the election.

12. Barack Obama, who is the president of the U.S., is from Chicago, Illinois.

13. Hanbock, which can be multicolored, is the traditional dress of Korea.

14. The counselor whom I saw advised me to take your class.

15. Kim Chi, which can be very hot, is a traditional Korean side dish.

Using Adjective Clauses to Identify a Person

Look for a student with a distinguishing characteristic and write a sentence with an adjective clause that other students in the class can use to identify the student about whom you wrote.

Read the sentence you wrote and have the students identify the person. Do not use a proper noun as the subject of the sentence.

Exercise 5.2

Change the second sentence in each pair to an adjective clause to modify the appropriate noun in the first sentence.

1. The students came late.
   The students missed the pop quiz.
   The students whom came late missed the pop quiz.

2. They missed the pop quiz.
   The pop quiz was easy.

if specific put comma
, which

They missed the pop quiz that was easy.

3. The pop quiz was easy.
   It was on adjective clauses.

on adj. clauses, was easy.
which was easy and

The pop quiz was easy which was on adjectives clauses.

4. The teacher was happy.
   His students understood adjective clauses.

understood Adj. clauses, was happy.

whose students
The teacher was happy that his students understood adjectives
who was happy   clauses.

5. The first day of class is the time.
   The teachers give a pre-test.

no commas because is specific.
when (time)

The first day of class is (the time) that the teachers give a
                                                         pre-test.

6. The placement test is given at the testing center.
   Makeup tests are also given at this place.

The placement test is given at the testing center whom
makeup tests are also given at this place.

7. The student is absent.
   He usually sits next to me.

The student who is absent usually sits next to me.

8. Another student sat next to me.
   His test was missing.

whose test was missing sat next to me.

Another student that sat next to me his test was
                                            missing.

9. The teacher came late.
   His car broke down on the way to school.

The teacher that came late his car broke down on the
whose   way to school. came
                                                         late

10. That car was relatively new.
    Its seats were made of leather.

That car which was relatively new its seats were
                        made of leather.
, whose seats were made of leather,
was relatively new

Exercise 5.3

Correct the mistake in the use of the adjective clause in each of the following sentences.

1. The student handbook, ~~who~~ *that* can be obtained for free, has important information.

2. The pre-test, that everyone must take, is a diagnostic test.

3. The teacher *who* is from Africa ~~whose~~ class I am taking, *his class*

4. Cell phones which are common these days, can be very annoying.

5. The librarian ~~to~~ who I returned the overdue books asked me to pay a fine.

6. The money is for tuition which he received from his father.

✓ 7. The lady who her twin sister is also taking the class is absent today.

✓ 8. The neighborhood where I live in is noisy.

✓ 9. The street which I live is busy during rush hour.

✓ 10. The man whom gave me a ride is my next door neighbor.

Exercise 5.4

Punctuate the following sentences if necessary.

1. A community college which is a two-year institution of higher learning offers credit and non-credit courses.

2. The e-mail that you sent last week must have been lost in cyberspace.

3. A kora which is a West African musical instrument has twenty one strings.

4. The CD which I got for Christmas was just what I wanted.

5. Junk food which is popular with kids is not good for them.

6. Running a red light which is a traffic violation can be dangerous.

7. The person whose cellular phone I found is in my freshman composition class.

8. My dad whose car broke down could not pick me up yesterday.

9. The person from whom I received a letter was my classmate.

10. My ESL 31 class which meets two days a week is interesting.

UNIT SIX
Cause and Effect

OBJECTIVES

By the end of this unit, you should be able:

- ■ to distinguish between cause and effect

- ■ to construct cause effect sentences

- ■ to construct the concluding sentence of a cause effect paragraph

- ■ to explain causal relationships

- ■ to use modal auxiliaries in cause effect sentences

- ■ to compose and edit a rough draft of a cause effect paragraph

---

PART I: THE CAUSE AND EFFECT PARAGRAPH

In a cause and effect paragraph, the writer may discuss why something happened (the cause(s)) or the result of an action, (the effect(s)). For example, if you set the alarm incorrectly, such an action can have a number of consequences or effects. Suppose you set the alarm incorrectly, your mistake could result in oversleeping, being late for work, missing an appointment and the like, all of which would be effects caused by your action. A paragraph that is about your reasons for oversleeping, being late for work, and missing an appointment focuses on cause; on the other hand, a paragraph that discusses what happened as a result of setting the alarm incorrectly focuses on effects.

In a cause and effect paragraph, the writer needs to not only state the causes or effects but also explain the causal relationship. In other words, how something leads to an outcome ought to be shown. For example, in explaining how bad weather can cause an accident, one may explain the process by which the cause leads to the effect. Furthermore, the writer may give examples that illustrate the causal relationship, and if possible, state the frequency of accidents due to bad weather.

Activity 6.1

Paragraph Analysis

Read the paragraph below and answer the questions that follow.

Using a cell phone while driving may lead to an accident. To begin with, when a driver wants to use a cell phone, he has to dial the number, and to do that, he needs to use at least one hand. Therefore, he cannot hold on to the steering wheel with both hands. In case of an emergency which may call for the use of both hands, he may not be able to act accordingly, and this can result in an accident. Furthermore, when a driver is on the phone, he may be deeply involved in the conversation and not paying full attention to other cars, traffic signals, and even pedestrians. For instance, if a traffic light turns red and a driver on the phone does not stop, he may be hit by other drivers who have right of way. A driver has to be alert at all times. As you can see, driving while using a cell phone can cause an accident; therefore, to avoid causing an accident, people must refrain from using a cellular phone while driving.

Paragraph analysis

a. Does the paragraph have a topic sentence?
b. Is the topic sentence at the beginning of the paragraph?
c. Does the topic sentence provide a cause of an accident?
d. Does the paragraph explain the causal relationship?
e. Does the paragraph include anecdotes?
f. Does the paragraph have a conclusion?
g. Does the conclusion restate the topic sentence or suggest ways to avoid accidents?

PART II: ELEMENTS OF A CAUSE AND EFFECT PARAGRAPH

Activity 6.2

The Topic Sentence of a Cause and Effect Paragraph

In a cause and effect paragraph, you either write about one cause that leads to a specific outcome or the consequence of an action. The topic sentence of a paragraph that discusses the cause of an accident is, therefore, comprised of the effect, an accident, and a possible cause the writer believes may lead to such an accident.

TASK   The topic sentence of a cause and effect paragraph is basically a cause effect statement. Complete the following topic sentences with a cause or effect.

1. Traffic accidents can be caused by _____.

2. Traffic accidents can be brought about by _____.

3. Speeding may lead to _____.

4. As a result of driving under the influence of alcohol, he had an_____.

5. He was texting; as a result, he had an _____.

Activity 6.3

Support Sentences of a Cause and Effect Paragraph

In writing a cause effect paragraph, you are expected to explain the causal relationship. In other words, how does the cause lead to the outcome? If, for example, you have speeding as a possible cause of accidents, you have to explain how going fast causes an accident. You may also give a personal experience or an accident you witnessed as an example.

TASK   In general terms, explain the causal relationship in the cause effect statements in activity 6.2 above.

Example

Cause effect statement: The accident occurred because the driver fell asleep.

Explanation of causal relationship in general terms: When a driver falls asleep, he is no longer in control of the car. As a result, he can hit another car or other objects.

Cause effect statement: _____

Explanation of causal relationship in general terms: _____

_____

_____

_____

_____

Cause effect statement: _____

Explanation of causal relationship in general terms: _____

_____

_____

_____

_____

Cause effect statement: _____

Explanation of causal relationship in general terms: _____

_____

_____

_____

_____

Cause effect statement: _____

Explanation of causal relationship in general terms: _____

_____

_____

_____

_____

Cause effect statement: _____

Explanation of causal relationship in general terms: _____

_____

_____

_____

_____

Activity 6.4

The Concluding Sentence

The concluding sentence of a cause and effect paragraph can be a statement that suggests how to prevent the effect from taking place if it is undesirable. For example, no one wants an accident; therefore, a paragraph that discusses the cause of an accident may end with a statement that tells the reader what has to be done to prevent such an accident from happening. On the other hand, a cause and effect paragraph may discuss the cause of a desirable effect; in which case, the conclusion may state what one can do to achieve or maintain the desirable effect. For example, if a paragraph discusses the cause of an improvement in the economy, the concluding sentence may suggest what has to be done for the continuation of this desired effect to occur.

TASK   Write a possible conclusion for a paragraph that develops each of the following topic sentences.

1. Speeding leads to an accident.

   Conclusion: _____

   _____

2. Driving while intoxicated can lead to an accident.

   Conclusion: _____

   _____

3. Being well-informed and the improving of one's language skills are two effects of watching television.

   Conclusion: _____

   _____

4. Driving in bad weather results in an accident.

   Conclusion: _____

   _____

5. He partied all night, so he failed the final exam the next morning.

   Conclusion: _____

   _____

6. Attending class regularly, taking good notes and studying can lead to success in school.

   Conclusion: _____

   _____

7. Drivers over the age of 80 cause accidents.

   Conclusion: _____

   _____

8. People who use a cell phone while driving cause accidents.

   Conclusion: _____

   _____

PART III: WRITING YOUR CAUSE AND EFFECT PARAGRAPH

Activity 6.5

Generating Ideas

TASK 1 In this unit, you will work on writing a paragraph about the causes of traffic accidents. One way to get ideas about the causes of traffic accidents is to recall and write brief descriptions of accidents. These anecdotes may be divided into three categories: (a) accidents you were involved in, (b) accidents you have witnessed, and (c) accidents you have heard about from a friend, read in the newspaper, seen on television, etc. These descriptions may be in the form of a free writing activity. In other words, do not worry about spelling and punctuation; just write a brief description of what you remember. If you are fortunate enough to not have been involved in an accident, (knock on wood) write about accidents you have witnessed or heard about, read, or seen on television.

1. Accident(s) I was involved in

2. Accident(s) I witnessed

3. Accident(s) I heard about

Determining Causes of Accidents

TASK 2 Determine one word or phrase as possible cause of the accident in each anecdote. A single phrase that characterizes the cause of an accident by an aggressive driver can be: "aggressive driving or aggressive driver."

Word or phrase as cause of anecdote one: _____

Word or phrase as cause of anecdote two: _____

Word or phrase as cause of anecdote three: _____

Activity 6.6

More Anecdotes

TASK   The following are rough drafts of sample anecdotes from students in low-intermediate ESL classes. Read each anecdote carefully and give a word or phrase as possible cause of the accident. The first one has been done for you.

Cause and Effect Anecdotes

1. *I was going to work at that time, and I was tired from the day before. I forced myself to drive and come to work because they needed my help so badly. I didn't realize that I fell asleep for a second and I hit the car right in front of me. The car was stopped at the stop sign. I was surprised and scared that time.*

    J.S.

    Word or phrase as possible cause of accident: Falling asleep while driving

2. *Three months ago I had an accident on the freeway. On that day, it was snowing and a lot of cars were stuck at the exit. I didn't know about it. I was driving fast so I stepped on the brake to reduce my speed, but I could not control the car. So I hit someone's car.*

    L.D.

    Give a word or phrase as possible cause of accident:

3. *Nine months ago, my older brother took me out to practice driving. While I was driving, there were a lot of cars at the intersection. I was exhausted and nervous. I stepped on the gas instead of the brake. I hit the street sign, but I didn't hit anybody.*

C.V.

Give a word or phrase as possible cause of accident:

4. *My sister was driving and she had to cross the main road, but she had to stop and wait until the road was clear. She said she saw a white car come from the right but she said it was far away so she had time to cross the street, but she didn't. When she saw the white car near her, she got nervous and stepped on the brakes and waited for the crash.*

M.S.

Give a word or phrase as possible cause of accident:

5. *It was around 12:00 P.M., and it was sunny, but the traffic wasn't heavy. I was driving on Route 7 with my sister. The speed limit was 45 mph. I was coming down hill and all of a sudden I saw a truck crossing the road a short distance away. So I pressed the brake and beeped the horn, but he didn't move. I did all I could do to stop the car, but he wouldn't move, so I hit him on the right side. My car was damaged, but his car was okay. He called the police and the police asked me if I was okay. I was nervous and scared because that was my first accident. We exchanged insurance information. The next day I had back pain, and I had pain in my neck. I called my insurance and told them.*

M. M.

Give a word or phrase as possible cause of accident:

6. *Last year I was driving on a country road. I was too sleepy, but I had a very important appointment the next morning. I fell asleep and lost control of the car. The car went different direction, and when it went over a hole, I woke up due to the vibration and tried to take control of the car. Even though I stepped on the brakes many times, the car hit a tree. Luckily, nobody was injured because we all had our seatbelts on and I wasn't driving too fast. Because of my sleepy condition I didn't press the gas hard.*

M

Give a word or phrase as possible cause of accident:

7. *I had an accident in 2001. It was almost 3:00 A.M. All my family was in the car. It was near my home. There were three police cars too. We were all stopped at a red light. The car came and hit my car. The car jumped to the other side. The police came and said, "Oh my goodness, thank god you guys are alive." My car went straight to the trash can. Since that day I have neck pain. And my dad has back pain. But we didn't go the hospital. They were speeding. Also his family went out and the son took the car without his parents' permission.*

O.N.

Give a word or phrase as possible cause of accident:

8. *I had an accident two months ago. I was driving through the green light, but another car went through the red light and crashed into my car. The other driver wasn't paying attention to the light and hit the back of my car. Because of that I had to do lots of insurance paperwork.*

S.D.

Give a word or phrase as possible cause of accident:

9. *Long time ago when I worked at Roy Roger's I saw a girl waiting for a ride. Sometimes she was there for at least an hour, then one day I was ready to go home. I asked her if she needs a ride and she said yes please. So I took her, but after she got in her apartment, I was leaving the place when suddenly a car hit me. This guy didn't check before leaving from the parking lot. I tried to avoid the accident but I couldn't. I didn't know this girl's apartment so I can use her phone to call, then waiting for the police and call my house and let my family know where I am or what happened. It took me more than two hours, so I got home around 11:00 P.M. The next day I was supposed to call my insurance and fix my car, etc. So to help that girl it took me so much time to resolve the accident I was involved.*

D.

Give a word or phrase as possible cause of accident:

10. *I was driving about 70 mph on the highway in New Jersey. There were three other people in my car which made my car a little heavy. A jeep just got on the highway; it was in front of me. The jeep changed two lanes to the left at once. Due to the slow speed of that car, I couldn't stop and crashed into it.*

J.C.

Give a word or phrase as possible cause of accident:

11. *Five years ago, I had a car accident. I was driving on the left lane on a highway with very high speed when suddenly a truck on the right was speeding with me and pulling me over the sidewalk. My car turned in a way that I had to drive only on the two right tires until the truck had passed me. After that my car stopped in the middle of the highway, and the truck just continued ahead. The front part of my car was broken, but for luck I wasn't hurt.*

Give a word or phrase as possible cause of accident:

12. *A long time ago, I was coming home from work rushing to get to my parents' house to get my son. I was driving a little fast and suddenly I hit a kid; he was on his bicycle. He had a stop sign, but he didn't stop. He ran in front of my car. I tried to avoid the accident, but I could not do it because he was fast and I was too. Luckily, he didn't die, but he had lots of broken bones.*

S.

Give a word or phrase as possible cause of accident:

13. *I was involved in an accident; it was raining and I was driving very slowly suddenly the light turned red, so I stopped. The car behind me was driving fast so he hit me from the back. What happened is we stopped and I get out of the car to see what happened to the car. It was a little scratch so I let him go. He was so sorry.*

Give a word or phrase as possible cause of accident:

14. *I was going straight on Little River Turnpike and an old lady without paying attention to the traffic light went through the red light and hit my car and my car got totaled and that time they took me to the hospital. I was in the hospital for one night and I must do surgery on my knee. The effect of that accident was I lost my knee and I never can run like before.*

Y.S.

Give a word or phrase as possible cause of accident:

Activity 6.7

Possible Causes of Accidents

TASK   The following words and phrases are often used in relation to traffic accidents. Discuss them to familiarize yourself with their meanings and usage. Add other words or phrases you know.

Falling asleep
Careless drivers
Negligent drivers
Reckless drivers
Inclement weather
Bad weather
Inexperienced drivers
Inattentive drivers
Speeding
Elderly drivers
Drunk drivers
Driving while impaired by alcohol / drugs
Drunken driving
Driving under the influence (DUI) of alcohol / drugs
Driving while intoxicated (DWI)
Distracted pedestrians
Truck drivers
Running a red light
Cell phone users
Defective cars
Aggressive drivers
Teenagers
Nervous drivers
Scared drivers

_____

_____

_____

_____

Activity 6.8

Analysis of Cause Effect Sentences

TASK 1 Study the following sentences carefully. The causes are in boldface, the effects are in italics, and the words or phrases that connect them are underlined.

1. **Inexperienced drivers** <u>cause</u> *accidents.*

2. **Driving under the influence of alcohol** <u>results in</u> *an accident.*

3. **Speeding** <u>leads to</u> *an accident.*

4. **He was talking on his cell phone;** <u>as a result,</u> *he had an accident.*

5. *The accident* <u>was due to</u> **his inattentiveness.**

6. <u>As a result of</u> **the icy road,** *I had an accident.*

7. *She had an accident* <u>because</u> **she was nervous.**

8. *The fatal accident* <u>was brought about by</u> **his driving while intoxicated.**

9. *The accident* <u>was caused by</u> **an elderly driver.**

10. **He was driving too fast;** <u>consequently,</u> *he had an accident.*

11. **He fell asleep;** <u>thus,</u> *he had an accident.*

12. *He had an accident,* <u>for</u> **he was driving under the influence of drugs.**

13. <u>Because</u> **he was driving while impaired by drugs,** *he had an accident.*

14. **He was driving fast on an icy road,** <u>so</u> *he had an accident.*

As you can see in the sentences above, the causes, effects, and connectors can be in different parts of a sentence. It is important to note what comes after the connector. A connector may be followed by a noun, noun phrase, or a complete sentence.

TASK 2 For each of the sentences above, give the structure that comes after the connector. The first two are examples.

1. Connector: Cause

   Followed by: <u>Noun</u>

2. Connector: Results in

   Followed by: <u>Noun phrase</u>

3. Connector: Leads to

   Followed by: _____

4. Connector: As a result

   Followed by: _____

5. Connector: Was due to

   Followed by: _____

6. Connector: As a result of

   Followed by: _____

7. Connector: Because

   Followed by: _____

8. Connector: Was brought about by

   Followed by: _____

9. Connector: Was caused by

   Followed by: _____

10. Connector: Consequently

    Followed by: _____

11. Connector: Thus

    Followed by: _____

12. Connector: For

    Followed by: _____

13. Connector: Because

   Followed by: _____

14. Connector: So

   Followed by: _____

Activity 6.9

Punctuating Cause Effect Sentences

TASK 1   Review the punctuation of the cause effect sentences in activity 6.8 and do the exercise below.

List the connectors that are preceded by a semicolon and followed by a comma.

    A. Conjunctive adverb or adverb phrase

        1. _____

        2. _____

        3. _____

Conjunctive adverbs such as the ones above connect two complete sentences. They are preceded by a semi-colon and followed by comma.

List the connectors that are preceded by a comma.

    B. Coordinators

        1. _____

        2. _____

        3. _____

The coordinators connect two complete sentences and are preceded a by comma.

List the verbs or verb phrases that connect the cause to the effect.

     C. Verbs or verb phrase

        1. _____

        2. _____

        3. _____

The verbs connect the subject, which may be the cause or the effect, to the object, cause or effect.

List the connectors that are at the beginning of a sentence or in the sentence but have no punctuation immediately before or after the connector.

     D. Subordinators

        1. _____

        2. _____

        3. _____

The subordinators form subordinate clauses or subordinate phrases. If the clause or phrase with the connector begins the sentence as in sentence 13 of activity 6.8, there is a comma at the end of the phrase. However, if the clause with the connector comes at the end of the sentence as in sentence 7 of activity 6.8, there is no comma.

TASK 2 Punctuate the following sentences if necessary.

    1. Since he was driving under the influence of alcohol he had an accident.

    2. He was not paying attention therefore he hit the car in front of him.

    3. Truck drivers cause accidents.

    4. Using a cell phone may lead to an accident.

    5. The accident happened as a result of his carelessness.

    6. The accident was caused by an elderly driver.

    7. He was reading the newspaper while driving as a result he had an accident.

    8. As a result of his aggressive driving he has many accidents.

9. Thanks to the cell phone traffic accidents have increased.

10. He ran a red light thus he hit another car.

Activity 6.10

Cause Effect Statements

TASK   Reread the student anecdotes in activity 6.6 and summarize each anecdote into a single cause effect statement. Use the connectors in task 1 of activity 6.9 above. Try to use each of them at least once. The first one has been done for you as an example.

1. The accident occurred **as a result of** the driver falling asleep.

2. _____

3. _____

4. _____

5. _____

6. _____

7. _____

8. _____

9. _____

10. _____

11. _____

12. _____

13. _____

14. _____

Activity 6.11

Modal Auxiliaries in Cause Effect Sentences

Cause effect sentences may include a modal auxiliary. This is particularly the case in statements of possibility as in: Drivers who are under the influence of alcohol **can** cause an accident. The modal auxiliary "**can**" in this sentence signifies possibility.

TASK   Underline the modal auxiliary in the following sentences and state the meaning it conveys. You may see the enabling grammar exercises on modals in this unit for help.

1. Negligent drivers can cause accidents.

2. Driving under the influence of alcohol may lead to an accident.

3. Inexperienced drivers must not drive in bad weather.

4. Senior citizens over 80 should not be allowed to drive.

5. The truck driver may have caused the accident.

6. The use of cell phones while driving should be banned.

7. He couldn't have caused the accident, for he was out of the country.

8. Inexperienced drivers ought not drive in bad weather.

9. Because he was driving under the influence of alcohol, he could have caused an accident.

10. Pedestrians who jaywalk may get hit.

Writing Assignment

1. Write a paragraph in which you discuss a possible effect of texting while driving.
2. Write a paragraph in which you discuss a possible cause of success in learning a second language.

PART IV: ENABLING GRAMMAR EXERCISES

Modals

Modals are very important, for they add meaning to a verb. For example, when one says, "I may go to the movies," he is expressing possibility; however, if he says "I would rather go to the movies," he is stating preference. The same action is stated in both cases, but the modals have added a specific meaning in each case. The following chart shows modals and the meanings they express.

The auxiliary "will" is also used as a modal to signify determination. For example, when a student says, "I will do my best next semester," he is not only talking about an action in the future, but he is also expressing determination to do his best.

Modal	Meaning	Example
Will	determination	I will maintain my 3.5 GPA.
Can	ability	I can drive.
Should	advice	You should see a doctor.
Must	obligation	I must attend the meeting.
Would rather	preference	I would rather stay home than go to the movies.
Had better	warning	You had better study, or you will fail.
May	possibility	I may transfer to a four-year college next year.
Be supposed to	expected behavior	You are supposed to attend class regularly.

Modals and Their Meanings

Exercise 6.1

The following sentences are, for example, about a student who wants to attend your school or program. Complete each sentence with the appropriate modal that corresponds to the meaning in parentheses.

1. (Ability) He _____ register by phone.

2. (Advice) He _____ register early.

3. (Warning) He _____ pay the tuition right away.

4. (Possibility) He _____ attend classes in the morning or in the afternoon.

5. (Warning) He _____ study.

6. (Ability) He _____ register in person.

7. (Obligation) He _____ attend classes.

8. (Advice) He _____ see a counselor if he needs advice.

9. (Possibility) He _____ join a study group.

10. (Ability) He _____ e-mail his writing assignments.

Negative Modals

The negative forms of modals are also used; for example, someone can be advised to do something or not to do something. The negative is formed by placing the negative marker "not" followed by the base form of the verb after the modal.

Exercise 6.2

Change the following sentences to negative.

Example

You **should not go** to the movies.

1. You had better go grocery shopping.

   _____

2. You should go to Shoppers Food Warehouse.

   _____

3. You must use cash to pay for the groceries.

   _____

4. You may leave now.

   _____

5. You can buy alcohol.

_____

6. I would rather go to Giant.

_____

7. I will be back before noon.

_____

8. We should buy enough groceries to last for a week.

_____

9. You should pay for the groceries by credit card.

_____

10. You may leave the groceries in the car while shopping at the mall.

_____

Modals in the Past Tense

The past forms of modals are structured in different ways. Study the past forms of the modals below. Note that some modals require the auxiliary "have" followed by the past participle of the verb and others do not.

Modal	Past form
Can	Could
Should	Should have
Must	Had to
May	Might
Would rather	Would rather have
Be supposed to	Was/were supposed to

Exercise 6.3

Change the following sentences from present to past.

Example

You should see a doctor.
You should have seen a doctor.

1. I can drive home with the groceries.

   _____

2. I would rather go shopping on Saturday.

   _____

3. You must empty the trunk.

   _____

4. I am supposed to go shopping.

   _____

5. I should keep the receipt.

   _____

6. I should pay by check.

   _____

7. I must bring the receipt with me.

   _____

8. I can go with him.

   _____

9. You are supposed to buy milk.

   _____

10. You should check the receipt before you leave the store.

    _____

11. I have to work hard.

    _____

Other Uses of Modals

Modals are also used for permission, request, politeness, and to portray other meanings.

Below are modals, possible meanings, and sample sentences.

Modal(s)	Meaning	Example
May Can Could	Permission	May I leave early? Can I go on the field trip? Could I use your phone?
Can Could Would	Request	Can you please take me to work? Could you please give me your phone number? Would you please give me a hand?
Could Would	Polite request	Could you please make less noise? Would you please give her your seat? Would you mind if I closed the door? Would you mind closing the door?
Could have	Action not taken, but too late	I could have taken the bus to school, but I didn't.
Couldn't have	Action that was apparently not possible	I couldn't have been in your class in 1988, for I was not born then.
Would have	Action not taken	I would have given you a ride if I had known.
Should have	Action not taken; some regret implied	I should have studied for the test.
Must	A good guess in the present based on what is known/ deduction	Juan was born and raised in Mexico, so he must speak Spanish.
Must have	A good guess or logical conclusion based on what is known	Joseph must have gone home because he said that he wasn't feeling well.

Exercise 6.4

Complete each of the following sentences with the appropriate form of the given modal and verb. Pay attention to the tense and whether or not you need the modal to be in the positive or negative form.

1. Kim _____ (should / register) for fifteen credits last semester.

2. Mustapha _____ (can / take) the test yesterday; he was out of town.

3. Joseph _____ (would rather / be) at home sleeping right now than doing this exercise.

4. I _____ (can / be) in your class in 1966; I wasn't born then.

5. John said that he wasn't feeling well; he _____ (must / go) home. He is nowhere to be found.

6. Susan has never been absent, but she is not here today; she _____ _____ (must / be) sick.

7. You _____ (had better / study) for the test; otherwise, you will fail.

8. You _____ (had better / take) I-66 at this time; it is HOV and you will be the only one in your car. You will get a ticket.

9. I have no idea where he is; he _____ (may / be) at home or at work.

10. Patel speaks Hindi; he _____ (must / be) from India.

UNIT SEVEN
Comparison and Contrast

OBJECTIVES

By the end of this unit, you should be able:

- ■ to determine if given items can be compared and whether to focus on similarities or differences

- ■ to construct a topic sentence, support sentences, and a concluding sentence of a comparison and contrast paragraph

- ■ to describe two approaches: one based on items being compared and the other based on specific areas or points of comparison

- ■ to use conjunctions

- ■ to compose and edit a rough draft of a comparison and contrast paragraph

---

PART I: THE COMPARISON AND CONTRAST PARAGRAPH

Comparison is about similarities and contrast is about differences. One can show what two people, places, or objects have in common, particularly cases in which the intended audience is familiar with one but does not know much about the other. Such paragraphs are on similarities. On the other hand, paragraphs that focus on contrasts emphasize differences. Differences are used to show what a person, place, or object is not. In so doing, the audience is made aware of the distinguishing characteristics of the two items being compared.

Items compared and/or contrasted usually have both similarities and differences. There may be more similarities than differences or vice versa. You cannot compare items that have nothing in common.

In this unit, you will use comparison and contrast to develop a paragraph.

Types of Comparison and Contrast Paragraphs

A comparison and contrast paragraph can be in one of two different formats. One is the type of paragraph in which the writer concentrates on one subject at a time by discussing its features, characteristics or ideas related to it first, and then shifts to discussions of the same issues with respect to the other subject. The other type is one in which the writer determines the quality or points on which to base the comparisons or contrasts and alternate between the subjects with respects to the quality or points in question. Below are examples of outlines, one of each type of paragraph. The paragraphs are comparison and contrast of rotary and cellular phones.

Type A: Approach Based on Items Being Compared or Contrasted

I. Rotary phone

Size

Mobility

Convenience

II. Cell phone

Size

Mobility

Convenience

Type B: Approach Based on Specific Areas or Points of Comparison

I. Size

Rotary phone

>   Big

Phone and receiver are separate pieces

Cell phone

>   Very small

Whole phone is one piece and can be held in one hand

Can be carried in a pocket or purse

II. Mobility

Rotary phone

>   Limited mobility based on length of wire or cord

Cell phone

>   Extensive mobility

III. Convenience or lack thereof

Rotary phone

Inconvenient—one has to go to the phone to make or receive a call

One has to walk to the phone to hang up

Cell phone

One can make or receive a call from anywhere

Activity 7.1

Paragraph Analysis

TASK   Read the following paragraph and answer the questions that follow.

Rotary phones and cellular phones are different in size, mobility and convenience or lack thereof. Rotary phones are relatively big compared to cellular phones. If we consider the main phone, receiver, and the cord, the rotary phone can easily be ten times the size of a cell phone and is therefore too bulky to put in a pocket. Not only is the rotary phone big, but it is also stationary. It is connected to wires, which makes it impossible to walk away with it. One has to go to the phone to make a call or to receive a call. In contrast, the cellular phone is so small that it can fit in the palm of one's hand. Due to the size of the cell phone, it can be taken anywhere; thus making it possible to make or receive a call from practically anywhere. For example, if one is stranded somewhere and has a cell phone, he or she can call for help. Because of its size, mobility, and convenience, the cell phone has become a very popular means of communication.

1. Does the paragraph have a topic sentence?
2. Is there a sentence that states the items being compared or contrasted and the points of comparison or contrast?
3. Does the paragraph focus on similarities or differences?
4. Is the approach based on items being compared or contrasted or specific areas of comparison or contrast?
5. Is there a concluding sentence? If so, what type of conclusion is it?

PART II: ELEMENTS OF A COMPARISON AND CONTRAST PARAGRAPH

Activity 7.2

The Topic Sentence

The topic sentence of a comparison and contrast paragraph is usually a statement that has the items to be compared or contrasted, a comparison or contrast verb or verb phrase, and it indicates whether or not the paragraph will focus on similarities, differences, or both. A topic sentence does not show or explain similarities or differences; it simply states that they exist and to what extent.

TASK 1 Study the following sentence patterns.

Comparison verbs or verb phrases:

1. Item 1 and item 2 + **be** + **similar** (+ Prep. Phrase).
   A rotary phone and touchtone phone **are similar** (in many ways).

2. **There** + **be** + **similarities** + between + item 1 and item 2.
   There are similarities between a rotary phone and a touchtone phone.

3. Item 1 and item 2 + **be** + **the same.**
   The receiver of a rotary phone and the receiver of a touchtone phone **are the same.**

Contrast verbs or verb phrases:

1. Item 1 and item 2 + **differ** (prep. Phrase).
   A rotary phone and a cellular phone differ in many ways.

2. Item 1 and item 2 + **be** + **different.**
   A rotary phone and a cellular phone **are different.**

3. **There** + **be** + **differences** + between + item 1 and item 2.
   There are differences between a rotary phone and cellular phone.

TASK 2 Write a topic sentence for a comparison and contrast paragraph on each of the following topics. Try to use a variety of patterns.

1. Topic: You and your teacher

   Topic sentence: _____

   _____

2. Topic: Your parents

   Topic sentence: _____

   _____

3. Topic: The house you live in and a house you lived in before

   Topic sentence: _____

   _____

4. Topic: Pets in the U.S. and pets in your country

   Topic sentence: _____

   _____

5. Topic: U.S. television programs and television programs in your country

   Topic sentence: _____

   _____

6. Topic: Two classes you are taking

   Topic sentence: _____

   _____

7. Topic: The weather where you live and another region of your choice

   Topic sentence: _____

   _____

8. Topic: Cats and dogs

   Topic sentence: _____

   _____

9. Topic: American music and the music of your country of origin

   Topic sentence: _____

   _____

10. Topic: The U.S. education system and the education system in your country

    Topic sentence: _____

    _____

Activity 7.3

Comparison and Contrast Support Sentences

Unlike topic sentences, which state the existence of similarities or differences between items, comparison and contrast support sentences show or explain similarities or differences. Such support sentences appear in many forms. Some, for example, are in the form of a compound sentence with two independent clauses and a connector. Others are complex sentences with a subordinate clause and an independent clause. Yet another type is one that has an independent clause and a phrase. This type of structure is a simple sentence. Below are commonly used comparison and contrast structures.

TASK 1 Study the following support sentences carefully.

A: **Contrast support sentences**

Type one: Transition words / phrases and coordinator

1. **A rotary phone is stationary;** however, **a cellular phone is portable.**
   (Contrast sentence)
   Other connectors used for this type of structure: In contrast
                                                       On the other hand

2. **A rotary phone is stationary,** but **a cellular phone is portable.**

Type two: Subordinators to form subordinate clause

1. *Whereas a rotary phone is stationary,* **a cellular phone is portable.**

Another connector used for this type of structure: While

Type three: To form subordinate phrase

1. *Unlike the rotary phone,* **the cellular phone is portable.**

Type four: Positioning contrast sentences side by side with semicolon, a connector, or a period

1. **A rotary phone is stationary; a cellular phone is portable.**
2. **A rotary phone is stationary, and a cellular phone is portable.**
3. **A rotary phone is stationary. A cellular phone is portable.**

B: **Comparison support sentences**

Type one: Transition words

>   1.   **A rotary phone has numbers and letters;** similarly, **a cellular phone has numbers and letters.**

Another connector used for this type of structure: Likewise

Type two: Subordinator to form subordinate clause

>   1.   **A rotary phone has numbers and letters** <u>just as a cellular phone does</u>.

Type three: Subordinator to form subordinate phrase

>   1.   *Similar to the rotary phone,* **the cellular phone has letters and numbers.**

Other connectors used for this type of structure: Like

Type four: Correlative conjunctions

>   1.   **Both rotary phones and cellular phones have numbers and letters.**
>   2.   **Not only rotary phones but also cellular phones have letters and numbers.**

(Note: These correlative conjunctions, not only . . . but also and both . . . and, are used to show what items have in common. Neither . . . nor can also be used to show similarity. For example, when you say "neither mom nor dad drives," you are saying that both of them don't drive, which is one thing they have in common.)

The structures in boldface are complete sentences or independent clauses. The underlined structures are dependent clauses, and phrases are in italics.

TASK 2 Use each pair of sentences to write a comparison and contrast support sentence. Vary your sentence types by writing simple, compound, and complex sentences.

>   1.   Jose speaks Spanish. Isamu speaks Japanese.

    _____

    _____

>   2.   Jose wears glasses. Isamu doesn't wear glasses.

    _____

    _____

3. Jose is an immigrant. Isamu is an immigrant.

_____

_____

4. Jose plays soccer. Isamu plays baseball.

_____

_____

5. Jose is Bolivian. Isamu is Japanese.

_____

_____

6. Isamu is shy. Jose is outgoing.

_____

_____

7. Jose is friendly. Isamu is friendly.

_____

_____

8. Jose has lived in the U.S. for one year. Isamu has lived in the U.S. for six months.

_____

_____

9. Jose is single. Isamu is married.

_____

_____

10. Jose is studying English as a Second Language at Northern Virginia Community College. Isamu is studying English as a Second Language at Northern Virginia Community College.

_____

_____

_____

_____

Activity 7.4

The Concluding Sentence

The conclusion of a comparison and contrast paragraph can be a restatement of the topic sentence. For instance, if a topic sentence states that there are differences between two objects, and the body of the paragraph discusses the differences, the concluding sentence can restate the topic sentence to reiterate the writer's opinion that there are indeed differences.

Another type of conclusion one can use is a summary sentence. Ending a paragraph with a summary sentence is an excellent way to help readers refocus; it puts all the supporting ideas into a single sentence. A summary sentence reminds the reader of the similarities and/or differences stated in the paragraph.

Other types of conclusions that can be used in a comparison and contrast paragraph are comments and predictions. In a paragraph that discusses similarities or differences that are likely to disappear in due course, the writer may make a comment or a prediction of what the two items will be like in the future.

TASK   Write a possible concluding sentence for a paragraph that develops each of the topic sentences.

1. My father and mother have different parenting styles.

   Concluding sentence: _____

   _____

   _____

2. A community college and a four-year college are different in many ways.

   Concluding sentence: _____

   _____

   _____

3. The approaches in the two classes I am taking this semester are totally different: one is methodical and the other is haphazard.

   Concluding sentence: _____

   _____

   _____

4. My brother and I are different in personality.

   Concluding sentence: _____

   _____

   _____

5. The U.S and my country celebrate national holidays in different ways.

   Concluding sentence: _____

   _____

   _____

6. Teenagers in the U.S. and teenagers in my country are different in a number of ways.

   Concluding sentence: _____

   _____

   _____

PART III: WRITING YOUR COMPARISON AND CONTRAST PARAGRAPH

Activity 7.5

Generating Ideas

When writing a comparison and contrast paragraph, the items being compared usually have not only similarities but also differences. There is no need to compare items that have nothing in common.

TASK Which of the following pairs do you think can be compared or contrasted? Give at least one similarity or difference if you think the items in a pair can be compared or contrasted.

Example

An umbrella and a mattress

   Can they be compared or contrasted?

   _____ Yes

   Similarity: _____

   Difference: _____

   __X__ No

A mattress and a futon

> Can they be compared or contrasted?
>
> __X__ Yes
>
> Similarity: Both used to sleep on
>
> Difference: A mattress is firm / a futon is not and can be folded and put away
>
> _____ No

1. A pen and an eraser

   > Can they be compared or contrasted?
   >
   > _____ Yes
   >
   > Similarity:_____
   >
   > Difference: _____
   >
   > _____ No

2. A pen and a pencil

   > Can they be compared or contrasted?
   >
   > _____ Yes
   >
   > Similarity:_____
   >
   > Difference: _____
   >
   > _____ No

3. Watching television and reading a book

   > Can they be compared or contrasted?
   >
   > _____ Yes
   >
   > Similarity:_____
   >
   > Difference: _____
   >
   > _____ No

4. An eraser and whiteout

   > Can they be compared or contrasted?
   >
   > _____ Yes
   >
   > Similarity:_____
   >
   > Difference: _____
   >
   > _____ No

5. The United States and food shopping in my country

   > Can they be compared or contrasted?
   >
   > _____ Yes
   >
   > Similarity:_____
   >
   > Difference: _____
   >
   > _____ No

6. Reading a book and listening to the radio

      Can they be compared or contrasted?

      _____ Yes

      Similarity:_____

      Difference: _____

      _____ No

7. A community college and a four-year college

      Can they be compared or contrasted?

      _____ Yes

      Similarity:_____

      Difference: _____

      _____ No

8. A car and a bicycle

      Can they be compared or contrasted?

      _____ Yes

      Similarity:_____

      Difference: _____

      _____ No

9. Halloween and Thanksgiving

      Can they be compared or contrasted?

      _____ Yes

      Similarity:_____

      Difference: _____

      _____ No

10. A computer and a typewriter

      Can they be compared or contrasted?

      _____ Yes

      Similarity:_____

      Difference: _____

      _____ No

Activity 7.6

Deciding What to Compare or Contrast

Some topics are too general and may have to be narrowed down to specific areas if you want to write a comparison and contrast paragraph on them. For example, if you were asked to compare or contrast your parents, you might decide to write about similarities or differences in parenting, appearance, personality, education, or professional experience.

TASK   The following topics are too general. Think of areas on which you can concentrate in writing a comparison and contrast paragraph and add them to those listed below each item.

1. Your country of origin and the United States
   Weather
   What is expected of a guest invited to dinner at someone's house?

   _____

   _____

   _____

2. Holidays in the United States and holidays in your country of origin
   National holidays

   _____

   _____

   _____

3. Buying and selling in two countries of your choice
   Buying a house
   Selling a house
   Grocery shopping

   _____

   _____

   _____

4. Transportation in the U.S. and in Korea
   Public transportation

   _____

   _____

   _____

5. American culture and Asian culture

_____

_____

_____

6. African tradition and Asian tradition

_____

_____

_____

7. Men and women

_____

_____

_____

8. The U.S. media and the media in my country
   Print media

_____

_____

_____

Activity 7.7

Deciding Whether to Compare or Contrast

Whether you choose to compare or contrast depends on your reason for writing your paragraph. For instance, a paragraph may focus on comparison if its purpose is to help the reader realize the similarities between an item they are familiar with and one that is new to them. On the other hand, a paragraph may focus on contrast if the two items have very few similarities and you want to emphasize the differences. Sometimes, students are given the same topic, but some choose to focus on similarities while others emphasize differences. For example, students in an intermediate writing class were given an assignment to write a paragraph in which they compare or contrast food shopping, food preparation, or meal times in their countries and in the U.S. Some students from western societies wrote about similarities, for as they claimed, they had more similarities than differences when it comes to food. Students from nonwestern countries, however, wrote about differences because, as one student put it, "As far as food is concerned, we have very little in common."

TASK   Read the following situations and decide whether you would focus on comparison or contrast.

1. You went to another country on vacation, and on your return, you want to write a paragraph to tell friends and family about the country you visited. You want them to know what the food, hospitality, shopping, or the weather is like in relation to the United States.

    Your focus:
    _____ Similarities
    _____ Differences

    Reason: _____

    _____

    _____

2. You want to convince your parents that it would be better to spend your first two years of post secondary education at a community college as opposed to a university.

    Your focus:
    _____ Similarities
    _____ Differences

    Reason: _____

    _____

    _____

3. You have seen two apartments that you really like, but you can't decide which one to rent. You want a friend or relative to help you decide between the two.

    Your focus:
    _____ Similarities
    _____ Differences

    Reason: _____

    _____

    _____

4. You are responding to a friend's request to recommend one of two movies you have seen.

   Your focus:
   _____ Similarities
   _____ Differences

   Reason: _____

   _____

   _____

5. You are asked to write a paragraph in which you compare or contrast food shopping, food preparation, and meal times in the United States and in your country of origin.

   Your focus:
   _____ Similarities
   _____ Differences

   Reason: _____

   _____

   _____

6. You are writing to a friend to let her know that it doesn't make any difference which in-state college she attends.

   Your focus:
   _____ Similarities
   _____ Differences

   Reason: _____

   _____

   _____

Activity 7.8

Listing Similarities and Differences

TASK 1 In order to write a comparison and contrast paragraph, it is important to know the similarities and differences between the items in question. Below are some differences between a rotary phone and a cell phone. Add more differences you can think of.

Rotary phone	Cell phone
Relatively big	Small
Stationary	Portable
Limited mobility	Mobile
Attached to wires	Wireless
Has a cord	Cordless
Rings	Chimes, beeps, or vibrates
Holes for finger to dial	Buttons to press for dialing
_____	_____
_____	_____
_____	_____
_____	_____
_____	_____

TASK 2 List the similarities you can think of between a rotary phone and a cell phone.

Rotary phone	Cell phone
Has letters and numbers for dialing	Has letters and numbers for dialing
_____	_____
_____	_____
_____	_____
_____	_____
_____	_____
_____	_____

When you compare or contrast two people, you may focus on appearance or personality. Below are similarities and differences a student came up with in comparing and contrasting herself and her teacher.

Differences

I	My teacher
Student	Teacher
Black hair	Salt and pepper hair
Bilingual	Multilingual
Female	Male
No glasses	Wears glasses
Shy	Not shy
Single	Married
Don't have Ph.D.	Ph.D.
Don't know grammar	Knows grammar
Work part-time	Works full-time

Similarities

English is my second language	English is his second language
An immigrant	An immigrant
Like rice	Likes rice
Live in Northern Virginia	Lives in Northern Virginia
Slim	Slim
Have a car	Has a car
Brown eyes	Brown eyes
Dimples	Dimples
Employed	Employed
Don't like cold weather	Does not like cold weather

TASK 3 Now list similarities and differences between you and another person.

A: Appearance

    You   **The other person**

    Similarities

_____   _____

_____   _____

_____   _____

_____   _____

_____   _____

    Differences

_____   _____

_____   _____

_____   _____

_____   _____

_____   _____

B: Personality

    Similarities

_____   _____

_____   _____

_____   _____

_____   _____

_____   _____

    Differences

_____   _____

_____   _____

_____   _____

_____   _____

_____   _____

TASK 4 Use the information in task 3 above to write a paragraph in which you compare yourself and the other person in appearance or personality.

Writing Assignment

1. Write a paragraph in which you compare food shopping in the United States and food shopping in your country of origin.
2. Write a paragraph in which you compare the weather in your country with that of the United States.

PART IV: ENABLING GRAMMAR EXERCISES

Coordinators

You need to use different types of sentences to make your writing more interesting. A paragraph with only simple sentences looks choppy, so it is better to also use compound, complex, and compound complex sentences in your paragraphs. In this chapter, we will study one way of forming compound sentences, i.e., the combination of two or more sentences.

Example

I like pizza. (simple sentence)

I hate spaghetti. (simple sentence)

I like pizza and spaghetti. (simple sentence)

I like pizza, but I hate spaghetti. (compound sentence)

To form a compound sentence, you must have at least two complete sentences that are properly connected. One type of connectors, coordinators, can be used to connect two or more sentences to form compound sentences. The coordinators are seven: *for, and, but, or, yet, so,* and *nor.*

Coordinators and the relationships they convey:

I am studying hard, for I want to pass the test. (For—reason)

I am tired, and I am sleepy. (And—more information)

I passed my English test, but I failed my math test. (But—contrast—opposite)

Every morning, I drink tea, or I drink coffee. (Or—choice)

He studies for his tests, yet he always fails them. (Yet—contrast—concession)

She goes to the beach, so she always has a tan. (So—result)

I don't drink tea, nor do I drink coffee. (Nor—two negatives)

(Note that there is a comma before the coordinator connecting the two complete sentences.)

Exercise 7.1

Form compound sentences with each given pair of sentences. Remember to use an appropriate coordinator and correct punctuation.

1. I will park in lot A.
   I will park in lot B.

   2. IC   I will park in lot A, or I will park in lot B ✓
   1 IC or: I will park in lot A or lot B. ✓

2. I don't have a bicycle.
   I don't have a car.

   I don't have a bicycle, and I don't have a car.

3. I like hot food.
   I use a lot of red pepper when I eat.

   I like hot food, so I use a lot of red pepper when I eat.

4. I watch American football.
   I don't understand it.

   I watch American football, but I don't understand it.

5. I am always late.
   I oversleep.

   I am always late, because I oversleep.

6. I call my family.
   I write to them.

   I call my family, so I write to them.

7. He takes notes.
   He can't read them.

   He takes notes, but he can't read them.

8. He has American friends.
   He has good oral skills.

   He has American friends, so he has good oral skills.

9. I go to McDonald's.
   I go to KFC.

   I go to McDonald's, or I go to KFC

10. I see her.
    She doesn't see me.

    I see her, but she doesn't see me.

Exercise 7.2

Some compound sentences may have more than two complete sentences. It is important to know how to connect many sentences; however, very long sentences must be avoided. Try connecting each group of sentences into one sentence. Make sure that you use appropriate connectors and correct punctuation.

1. I don't call my family.
   It is too expensive.
   I write to them.

   I don't call my family, because it is too expensive, but I write to them.

2. I am not close to a metro station.
   I don't have a car.
   I take the bus.

   I am not close to a metro station, and I don't have a car, so I take the bus.

3. I speak my language at home.
   I do not listen to the news on TV or the radio.
   I have poor listening skills.

   I speak my language at home, but I ; in addition, don't listen to the news on TV or the radio, so I have poor listening skills.

4. Bruce works at night.
   He goes to school during the day.
   He often falls asleep in class.

   Bruce works at night, and he goes to school ; also, during the day, so he often falls asleep in class.; therefore,

5. He comes to class every day.
   He studies hard.
   He gets good grades.

   He come to class every day. He studies hard, , and and he gets good grades. ; therefore,

Conjunctive Adverb or Adverb Phrase

You can form compound sentences with coordinators; likewise, you can form compound sentences by using conjunctive adverbs and correlative conjunctions.

Relationship	Coordinator	Conjunctive adverb or adverb phrase
More information	And	Moreover, furthermore, in addition
Contrast	But	On the other hand, however
Concession	Yet	Nevertheless
Result	So	As a result
Reason	For	–
Two negatives	Nor	–
Choice	Or	–
Example	–	For example, for instance
Emphasis	–	In fact
Similarity	–	Similarly, likewise

Exercise 7.3

Form compound sentences with the given pairs of sentences and conjunctive adverbs. Remember to use correct punctuation.

Example

I studied for the test; as a result, I passed it.

(In addition) I like baseball. I like soccer.

I like baseball; in addition, I like soccer.

(As a result) I had two tickets. I invited my friend to go to the game with me.

I had two tickets; as a result, I invited my friend to go to the game with me.

(Nevertheless) I was tired. I went to the game.

I was tired; nevertheless, I wen to the game.

(For example) I like Italian food. I like spaghetti and meatballs.

I like Italian food. For example, I like spaghetti and meatballs

(In fact) I went with them to the game. I was the one who drove them to the game.

I went with them to the game. In fact, I was the one who drove them to the game.

(Similarly) I saw the game on television. She saw the game on television.

I saw the game on TV. Similarly, she saw the game on TV.

(Likewise) I had a part-time job. He had a part-time job.

I had a part-time job. Likewise, He had a part-time job.

(On the other hand) I had a part-time job. He had a full-time job.

I had a part-time job. On the other hand, he had a full-time job.

Correlative Conjunctions

Other connectors that are used in compound sentences are correlative conjunctions. These two part connectors, except for "both...and," can be used to connect complete sentences. All correlative conjunctions, however, can connect equal elements such as verbs, nouns, adjectives, phrases, and clauses.

Not only ... but also (More information)	Not only did I play football, but I also played basketball.
	I played not only football but also basketball.
Neither ... nor (Two negatives)	I was neither a hockey player nor a soccer player. (Commonly used to form a simple sentence.)
	I played neither hockey nor soccer.
Either ... or (Choice)	Either I played football, or I played basketball.
	I played either football or basketball.
Both ... and (More information)	I play both football and basketball. (Not used to connect sentences.)

Exercise 7.4

Connect each pair of sentences with a correlative conjunction to form a compound sentence.

1. I was a basketball player.
   I was a football player.

   _____

   _____

   _____

2. I didn't play hockey.
   I didn't play cricket.

   _____

   _____

   _____

3. Hockey was a popular sport.
   Soccer was a popular sport.

   _____

   _____

   _____

4. We had tennis courts.
   We had basketball courts.

   _____

   _____

   _____

5. We could go to a football game.
   We could go to a volleyball game.

   _____

   _____

   _____

6. He could have been a professional soccer player.
   He could have been a professional baseball player.

   _____

   _____

   _____

7. Baseball is a team sport.
   Soccer is a team sport.

   _____

   _____

   _____

8. Football players wear protective gear.
   Hockey players wear protective gear.

   _____

   _____

   _____

9. I play ice hockey.
   I play field hockey.

   _____

   _____

   _____

10. Field hockey is not played on ice.
    Basketball is not played on ice.

    _____

    _____

    _____

UNIT EIGHT
Classification

OBJECTIVES

By the end of this unit, you should be able:

- ■ to describe the process of classification

- ■ to determine the principle by which to classify a group or entity you are familiar with

- ■ to construct classification sentences

- ■ to compose and edit a rough draft of a classification paragraph

---

PART I: THE CLASSIFICATION PARAGRAPH

Classification is used daily to make sense of what may look chaotic. As a rule, you probably try to put things at home in order. For example, you may sort things such as the mail, laundry, groceries, and even the garbage. If you have two or more people living at home, for instance, you may sort the mail according to addressees in the family. The laundry may also be sorted according to colors, type of fabric, cold, warm, or hot wash, etc. As for the groceries, they may have to be sorted a number of times. To begin with, they are sorted at the store in groups depending on whether they are perishable items, frozen, solid, or delicate items such as eggs. When you get home, you may have to sort them again to put them away in the freezer, refrigerator, vegetable tray, on the counter, in the bread basket, etc. Furthermore, many local governments in the United States require that their citizens sort their garbage and put paper, plastic, bottles, hazardous material, and biodegradable material in separate bins supplied by the local authorities. As you can see, whether you are conscious of it or not, you are always engaged in the process of classification.

Just as you classify objects, you can also categorize ideas. Ideas may be jumbled up in your head, and to make sense of them in order to write a coherent paragraph, you may first have to jot them down on paper and then put them in categories. The ability to classify is a necessary skill. In this unit, you will use the process of classification as a method of paragraph development.

Activity 8.1

Paragraph Analysis

Read the following paragraph and answer the questions that follow.

Immigrants in the United States can be categorized according to their status. Some immigrants are legal permanent residents. In other words, they have all the necessary papers to live and work in the United States. As green card holders, these non-citizens enjoy many privileges that citizens have. However, permanent residents cannot vote, nor can they apply for certain federal jobs. Other immigrants are undocumented. These people do not have the necessary papers, and are, therefore, not allowed to work. They face difficulties in finding employment, and a place to live. The third category of immigrants is made of those that are in process. They are people who have lived in the country for a while and have applied for permanent residency but are waiting for their papers. They have temporary documents with which they can apply for work. No matter their status, undocumented, legal, or in process, most immigrants are delighted to have made it to this land of opportunity.

1. Does the paragraph have a topic sentence?
2. What is the sum total being classified?
3. How many categories are discussed in the paragraph?
4. By what characteristics are the students classified?
5. Does the topic sentence give a specific number of groups?
6. In what order are the groups presented? Can you suggest another way of ordering the groups?
7. Does the paragraph have a conclusion?

PART II: ELEMENTS OF A CLASSIFICATION PARAGRAPH

Activity 8.2

The Topic Sentence of a Classification Paragraph

You must remember your topic sentence is the main idea of your paragraph, which is about classifying a sum total into categories. Your topic sentence should, therefore, suggest a specific number or quantifiers to show range of categories. It may also suggest method of categorizing and the direction the paragraph is set to be developed.

TASK   Read the following topic sentences and answer the questions that follow.

1. My classmates can be categorized into two groups depending on whether they are shy or outgoing.
    1. Does the topic sentence give the sum total or larger group to be classified?
    2. Does the topic sentence include a specific number of groups?
    3. Does the topic sentence have a quantifier instead of a specific number?
    4. By what characteristics are the classmates classified?
    5. How do you think a paragraph with this topic sentence will be developed?
    6. Does the topic sentence show tendency to a certain direction such as least interesting to most interesting?

2. Immigrants in the United States can be classified by their reason for emigrating.
    1. Does the topic sentence give the sum total or larger group to be classified?
    2. Does the topic sentence include a specific number of groups?
    3. Does the topic sentence have a quantifier instead of a specific number?
    4. By what characteristics are the classmates classified?
    5. How do you think a paragraph with this topic sentence will be developed?
    6. Does the topic sentence show tendency to a certain direction such as least interesting to most interesting?

3. My Arabic 101 class has students with varying degrees of proficiency: beginners, low-intermediate to high-intermediate, and native speakers.
    1. Does the topic sentence give the sum total or larger group to be classified?
    2. Does the topic sentence include a specific number of groups?
    3. Does the topic sentence have a quantifier instead of a specific number?
    4. By what characteristics are the classmates classified?
    5. How do you think a paragraph with this topic sentence will be developed?
    6. Does the topic sentence show tendency to a certain direction such as least interesting to most interesting?

Activity 8.3

Writing a Topic Sentence

TASK Write a topic sentence for each of the following items. Use the questions above to help you analyze each of the topic sentences you write.

1. Topic: Transportation in the United States

    Topic sentence: _____

    _____

    _____

    _____

    _____

2. Topic: Food in the United States

    Topic sentence: _____

    _____

    _____

    _____

    _____

3. Topic: Recreation activities in the United States

    Topic sentence: _____

    _____

    _____

    _____

    _____

Activity 8.4

Developing a Classification Paragraph

If you chose to categorize a whole into smaller groups, your focus shifts from the big picture to the smaller groups. The two or more groups may be viewed in different ways. For example, you may define each category, discuss the makeup of each group and attributes within each group, group dynamics, or relationship between groups.

Your paragraph may also address your reason for the grouping you came up with in your classification. Your topic sentence may suggest your plan of action, i.e., how your paragraph is to be developed. For example, the topic sentence above that categorizes the students based on whether they are shy or outgoing may be developed by discussing the behavior of the students in each group. The outgoing students may be those that tend to dominate while the others stay quiet or simply look on. Attributes of members of each of the groups ought to be discussed. That is why they are members of a given group in the first place.

The categorization of a larger group may also raise certain questions. Your paragraph may be developed to address those questions. For example, a paragraph that supports the topic sentence about the Arabic class with students of varying degrees of proficiency may include the reason why the native speakers are taking a class for beginners, attitudes and student participation.

TASK Read the following topic sentences and jot down questions you would want answered in a paragraph that supports the topic sentence. The first topic sentence has sample questions. Can you add more questions you would want answered?

1. My Arabic 101 class has students with varying degrees of proficiency: beginners, low-intermediate to high-intermediate, and native speakers.

    1. Why are the native speakers taking a class for beginners?
    2. What is the attitude of the students, both native and non-native speakers?
    3. Is there any disparity in classroom participation?
    4. Do the native speakers get bored?
    5. What are the advantages of having native Arabic speakers in an Arabic class for beginners?
    6. _____
    7. _____
    8. _____
    9. _____
    10. _____

2. Gangs in our town can be distinguished by one of three insignias that show their membership: a scorpion, a dragon, and a bow and arrow.

    1. _____
    2. _____
    3. _____

4. _____

5. _____

6. _____

7. _____

3. Immigrants in the United States can be classified by their reason for emigrating.

1. _____

2. _____

3. _____

4. _____

5. _____

6. _____

7. _____

4. Your topic sentence in the task of activity 8.3 about recreation activities in the United States.

1. _____

2. _____

3. _____

4. _____

5. _____

6. _____

7. _____

How your paragraph is developed may depend on your reasons for the categorization or questions your audience may have about the groups. In some cases, you may have to define concepts or group identity. For example, the topic sentence—"Immigrants in the United States may be divided into three categories: legal, undocumented, and in process," may require the writer to define the three categories, particularly "in process."

You may also choose to describe the makeup and function of each category. This may be true for topic sentences like the one above about the gangs. For instance, you may describe the members of each group and their respective activities. A paragraph about the gangs may also be developed by comparing or contrasting the various groups and their impact on the community.

Activity 8.5

Ordering of Categories

You may order the categories in your paragraph to reveal elements of surprise, go from least interesting to most interesting, least proficient to most proficient, or simply in chronological order. Some categories may be ordered based on more than one reason. For example, the ordering of the categories of the students taking the Arabic 101 is from least proficient to most proficient. However, the ordering also gradually reveals elements of surprise. Beginners are expected to be taking such a class, but not intermediate, and definitely not native speakers. Another more subtle way of revealing elements of surprise is to state the number of categories but introduce them piecemeal in the body of the paragraph.

TASK   Read the following topic sentences and suggest the type of ordering that may be used. Note that some topic sentences do not have categories listed; therefore, the type of ordering may be delayed to reveal an element of surprise.

1. Colleges distinguish between in-state tuition and out-of-state tuition.

    Type of ordering: _____

2. Immigrants can be categorized based on their status.

    Type of ordering: _____

3. Immigrants are of three types: undocumented, in process, and legal permanent residents.

    Type of ordering: _____

4. Countries can be classified into developed and developing.

    Type of ordering: _____

5. Gas station attendants distinguish between full service and self-service.

    Type of ordering: _____

6. Countries can be classified as first world, second world, and third world.

    Type of ordering: _____

7. Students in my ESL class can be categorized into three groups depending on when they get to class: those who come early, those who come on time, and those who come late.

Activity 8.6

The Concluding Sentence

The concluding sentence of a classification paragraph may be a restatement of the topic sentence with the principle and categories, a summary sentence, a comment, or a combination of two or all three. A concluding sentence which is a restatement reminds the reader of the principle by which you classified the subject and the categories. This kind of conclusion may be used in paragraphs whose topic sentence includes the categories and principle by which members of the larger unit or group are classified.

You may wish to make a comment as your concluding sentence based on the categories and support sentences in the body of the paragraph. For example, the concluding sentence of the paragraph about immigrants restates the categories followed by a comment that the immigrants are delighted to have made it to this country of opportunity irrespective of their status. The larger group, immigrants, is categorized into smaller groups—legal, undocumented, and in process,—but the comment is on a common interest; thus making the reader see the immigrants again as members of a larger group as opposed to members of subcategories. This concluding sentence is a combination of restatement and comment.

Restating a Topic Sentence

TASK 1 One way to restate a topic sentence is to change it from passive to active or vice versa. Change the following sentences from active to passive if possible. Remember, you can only change a sentence from active to passive if it has an object.

Example

Active: Public colleges and universities classify students as in-state or out-of-state students.

Passive: Students are classified as in-state or out-of-state by public colleges and universities.

Active: Public colleges and universities distinguish between in-state and out-of-state students.

Passive: Cannot be changed to passive.

1. One can classify tuition at public colleges and universities as in-state tuition or out-of-state tuition.

   _____

   _____

2. Counselors categorize international students into two groups: immigrant students and F1 (visa) students.

   _____

   _____

3. Colleges categorize their student body as freshman, sophomore, juniors, and seniors.

_____

_____

4. One can divide university employees into two groups: faculty and staff.

_____

_____

5. One can classify college holidays as religious, national, and institutional.

_____

_____

6. Community colleges offer credit courses and non-credit courses.

_____

_____

7. Colleges distinguish between adjunct faculty and full-time faculty.

_____

_____

8. One can classify my classmates into two groups depending on whether they are shy or outgoing.

_____

_____

9. Someone can classify immigrants in the U.S. by their reason for emigrating.

_____

_____

10. One can categorize immigrants based on their status.

_____

_____

TASK 2 Topic sentences with the anticipatory subject "there" can be restated with the real subject. Rewrite the following sentences using the real subject as opposed to the anticipatory subject. See example below.

Example

There are three types of registration offered by the college: Online registration, telephone registration, and in-person registration.

Online registration, telephone registration, and in-person registration are three types of registration offered by the college.

1. There are two kinds of gender based social organizations on college campuses: fraternities for men and sororities for women.

   _____

   _____

2. There are five types of parking on our campus: faculty and staff parking, student parking, visitor parking, metered parking, and motorcycle parking.

   _____

   _____

3. There are two categories of nations: developed and developing.

   _____

   _____

4. There are two types of service at gas stations: full service and self-service.

   _____

   _____

5. There are two types of food on college campuses: cafeteria food and snacks.

   _____

   _____

PART III: WRITING YOUR CLASSIFICATION PARAGRAPH

Activity 8.7

Generating Ideas

When you classify, you are in essence putting things, people, or ideas that have a predetermined characteristic in common in groups or categories. In other words, members of each category share the same criterion for being members of the group. As a writer, one of your tasks is to decide the characteristic by which to classify your subjects. There may be many distinguishing traits you can use; however, you have to choose one that helps you achieve the grouping you wish to address in your paragraph. For example, you can classify your classmates by gender, nationality, or personality. However, students learning English as a Second Language might be classified by reasons for taking the class or reasons for being in the country if you wish to address their motivation or reasons for immigrating to the host country.

TASK 1 Think of other principles by which you can classify the following subjects and add them to the list below each item.

Your classmates

    Gender

    Nationality

    Personality—shy / gregarious

    Language

    Reasons for studying English

    Reasons of immigrating to host country

    _____

    _____

    _____

    _____

    _____

Immigrants

    Country of origin

    Length of stay

    Status

    Reasons for immigrating

    _____

    _____

_____

_____

_____

Student body

    Gender

    Major

    Year—freshman, sophomore, junior, senior

    Instate / out of state

_____

_____

_____

_____

_____

Contents of your backpack or purse

    Books

    Writing implement

_____

_____

_____

_____

_____

Determining Principles for Classification

When you classify a large unit into categories, each member of the larger group must be accounted for. You must not leave an individual, object, place, or idea out because it doesn't belong in any of your categories. For example, if you classify the students in a class as freshmen and sophomore, but there is a student who is auditing the class, your classification does not take everybody in the larger group into account, for this student cannot be placed in any of the smaller groups. It is important to use a principle by which everybody can be classified.

Also, there has to be consistency in your system of classification. For instance, if you classify a group of students by nationality, you must make sure that every member of a category is in it because of his or her nationality. For example, if you classify a group by nationality and list the places they come from as Canada, the United States, and South America, you are not consistent in your classification. The United

States and Canada are nations, but South America is a subcontinent with many nations. To be consistent, you have to stick to your principle of classification and use the countries that group members come from.

Another common error in classification is when a member of the larger group can be in two or more categories. If, for instance, you classify your classmates into three groups depending on whether they are shy, observant, or outgoing, it is possible for someone to be shy and observant at the same time thus straddling the line between two categories. When members of a large group are classified, each member of the subgroups can only belong to one category.

Some of the features listed under each of the items in task 1 above may not be instructive. That is to say, we may not learn much from some of the groupings. For example, categorizing your classmates by gender may not be an important move unless there are remarkable differences in attitude, behavior, or distinct patterns portrayed strictly along gender lines.

TASK 2 Go over the characteristics listed under the items in task 1 above and put a check next to the ones you think are instructive or interesting enough to be developed in a paragraph. Next, write the item, the principle, and categories by which you wish to classify each one of them.

Example

Item:	Immigrants
Principle:	Status
Categories:	Legal, undocumented, in process

1. Item: _____

    Principle: _____

    Categories: _____

2. Item: _____

    Principle: _____

    Categories: _____

3. Item: _____

    Principle: _____

    Categories: _____

4. Item: _____

    Principle: _____

    Categories: _____

5. Item: _____

    Principle: _____

    Categories: _____

Activity 8.8

Writing Classification Sentences

TASK   Read the following sentences and identify what is being classified and into how many parts. The sentences are about colleges and universities.

1. Tuition at public colleges and universities can be classified as in-state tuition and out-of-state tuition.

   What is classified?_____

   Categories: _____

2. Counselors distinguish between immigrant students and F1 (visa) students.

   What is classified?_____

   Categories: _____

3. English language learners can be divided into two groups: English as a Second Language (ESL) students, who study in a country where English is the main language of communication, and English as a Foreign Language (EFL) students, who study English in their native countries, where English is not the main language of communication.

   What is classified?_____

   Categories: _____

4. There are three types of registration: Online registration, telephone registration, and in-person registration.

   What is classified?_____

   Categories: _____

5. College students are categorized as freshmen, sophomore, juniors, and seniors.

   What is classified?_____

   Categories: _____

6. College and university employees are of two types: faculty and staff.

   What is classified?_____

   Categories: _____

7. English as a Second Language programs offer four skill-areas: grammar, reading, writing, and speaking.

   What is classified?_____

   Categories: _____

8. Universities distinguish between campus residents and off-campus students.

   What is classified?_____

   Categories: _____

9. Subjects offered in colleges and universities are in the humanities and sciences.

   What is classified?_____

   Categories: _____

10. There are two kinds of gender based social organizations on college campuses: fraternities for men and sororities for women.

    What is classified?_____

    Categories: _____

11. There are five types of parking: faculty and staff parking, student parking, visitor parking, metered parking, and motorcycle parking.

    What is classified?_____

    Categories: _____

Activity 8.9

Punctuating Classification Sentences

A common classification sentence is one that has an introductory statement with a colon followed by categories. The categories listed after the colon may be two or more. If the categories are two, they are connected with a conjunction; however, if they are three or more, they become a series and are separated by commas. Read the two sample sentences below and pay attention to the punctuation.

1. There are five types of parking on our campus: faculty and staff parking, student parking, visitor parking, metered parking, and motorcycle parking,

2. There are two service options at gas stations: full service and self-service.

TASK Punctuate the following sentences if necessary by adding colons and commas.

1. College holidays are of three types religious national and institutional.

2. Students in my freshman composition can be categorized in to three groups based on when they come to class those who come early those who come on time and those who come late.

3. Compact cars can be classified according to number of doors two-door and four-door.

4. Community colleges offer credit courses and non-credit courses.

5. Colleges offer three types of financial aid grants loans and work study.

Activity 8.10

Classification Sentences in the Active Voice or Passive Voice

A classification sentence can be in the active voice or the passive voice. You may choose to write your classification sentence in the active voice if you want to emphasize the "doer" as opposed to the "person or thing" that received the action. The primary use of the passive voice, however, is to shift emphasis. The passive voice is, therefore, often preferred in cases in which the "doer" is either not known or is common knowledge. (See enabling grammar exercises at the end of this unit for more practice on changing sentence from active to passive.)

To change a sentence from active to passive, the sentence in the active must have a **subject, verb,** and an **object,** for these three elements form the essential parts of the sentence in the passive voice. The object of the active sentence becomes the subject of the passive sentence. Furthermore, the verb of the active sentence becomes a two-part phrase, the tense marker and the past participle of the main verb.

The modal auxiliaries "can" and "may" are often used in classification sentences. After all, when you divide or categorize things or people into smaller groups, you are showing that it can be done; thus the auxiliaries "can" and "may" are used to connote possibility. The subject of the active voice becomes part of a phrase, commonly called "by phrase" that indicates the "doer" if needed. When the modal auxiliaries "can" and "may" are used in the passive, the verb phrase of the passive sentence includes "**be,**" which is placed between the modal auxiliary and past participle of the main verb.

Study the active sentences and their corresponding passive sentences below. Pay attention to difference in sentence structure when a sentence is changed from active to passive. The subjects of the active sentences are underlined, the verbs are in bold, and the objects, if any, are in italics. The corresponding passive sentences show changes in the position of the active subject, verb or verb phrase, and object.

Active Sentence

1. <u>Community colleges</u> **offer** *credit courses and non-credit courses.*

2. <u>One</u> **can classify** *tuition at public colleges and universities* as in-state tuition and out-of-state tuition.

3. <u>Universities</u> **distinguish** between campus residents and off-campus residents.

4. <u>One</u> **can divide** *English language learners* into two groups: English as a Second Language (ESL) students and English as a Foreign Language (EFL) students.

Passive Sentence

1. *Credit courses and non-credit courses* **are offered** <u>by community colleges</u>.

2. *Tuition at public colleges and universities* **can be classified** as in-state tuition and out-of-state tuition.

3. Active sentence #3 above cannot be changed to passive, for it doesn't have an object.

4. *English language learners* **can be divided** into two groups: English as a Second Language (ESL) students and English as a Foreign Language (EFL) students.

Note that some classification sentences have a statement, a prepositional phrase, and the categories. The statement in such a sentence is what you can change from active to passive; the propositional phrase and the categories do not change. The prepositional phrase "into two groups" and the categories after the colon in the active sentence #4 do not change, i.e., they are the same in the active as well as the passive sentences. Also note that passive sentence #4 doesn't have a "by phrase" because the subject "one" does not provide important information.

TASK   Use the given information to form classification sentences. You may use the active or passive voice.

Example

faculty / adjunct, full-time
Faculty members can be divided into two groups: adjunct faculty and full-time faculty.

1.   Sports / indoor, outdoor

   _____

   _____

2.   Nations / developed, developing

   _____

   _____

3.   Sports / individual, team

   _____

   _____

4. Textbooks / fiction, non-fiction

   _____

   _____

5.   Countries / first world, second world, third world

   _____

   _____

6.   Workers in the U.S. / white collar, blue collar

   _____

   _____

7.   Food on college campuses / cafeteria food, prepared and served in cafeteria and snacks, sold in vending machines

   _____

   _____

Writing Assignment

1. Write a paragraph about people you have met in your town or neighborhood. You may wish to classify these people into specific groups. Make sure that the body of your paragraph supports the reason for your classification.

2. Workers in the United States are classified as white collar and blue collar. Write a paragraph in which you define these categories. Include examples of workers in each category and the type of work they do.

PART IV: ENABLING GRAMMAR EXERCISES

Passive Voice and Active Voice

A sentence may be better in the active voice if the speaker wants to emphasize the "doer" as opposed to the person or object that received the action. For example, if someone in a family who is not a very good cook surprises everyone because he made a delicious dish for dinner, then a sentence in the active voice that emphasizes the "doer" as in "**Michael made dinner**" would be appropriate. However, if someone ate the leftovers, but the "doer" is not known, then a sentence in the passive that emphasizes the leftovers, i.e., what happened to them would be preferred. Thus we may have a sentence such as "**The leftovers were eaten.**" The primary use of the passive voice is to shift emphasis. To give another example, if a homeless man was hit by someone on Main Street, a sentence reporting the accident might be: "A homeless man was hit on Main Street." The phrase, "by someone" is not necessary in this case because it doesn't give us new, important information. The passive voice is, therefore, often preferred in cases in which the "doer" is either not known or is common knowledge. The sentence: "The mailman delivered my mail at noon" may be stated in the passive voice as: My mail was delivered at noon. In this case, the "by phrase" may not be necessary because it is common knowledge that the mailman delivers the mail.

To change a sentence from active to passive, the sentence in the active must have a **subject, verb** and an **object,** for these three elements form the essential parts of the sentence in the passive voice. The object of the active sentence becomes the subject of the passive sentence. Furthermore, the verb of the active sentence becomes a two-part phrase, the tense marker and the past participle of the main verb. The subject of the active voice becomes part of a phrase, commonly called "by phrase" that indicates the "doer" if needed. See diagram below.

Active sentence

Mike	makes	dinner.
(Subject)	(Verb)	(Object)

Passive sentence

Dinner	is	made	by Mike
(Subject)	(Tense marker)	(Past participle)	(By phrase)

Below are the passive forms of the same sentence in the twelve tenses. It is important to note that the only column that looks different is the "tense marker" column. Every other column has the same word or phrase for all the tenses. It is also important to note that when a sentence is changed from active to passive, the tense doesn't change. The only changes that occur are that the person, place, or thing that received the action is placed in the subject position, and if necessary, the "doer" is moved to the end of the sentence and turned into a phrase that includes the word "by."

Subject		Tense marker	Past participle	By phrase
Singular Dinner	*S. Present*	is	made	by Mike.
Plural Dinners		~~are~~		
Dinner	*Present Progres*	is being	made	by Mike.
Dinner	*Present Perfect*	has been	made	by Mike.
~~Dinner~~		~~has been being~~	~~made~~	~~by Mike.~~
Dinner	*S. Past*	was	made	by Mike.
Dinner	*Past Progresive*	was being	made	by Mike.
Dinner	*Past perfect*	had been	made	by Mike.
~~Dinner~~		~~had been being~~	~~made~~	~~by Mike.~~
Dinner	*Future*	will be	made	by Mike.
~~Dinner~~		~~will be being~~	~~made~~	~~by Mike.~~ *skip*
Dinner	*Future Perfect*	will have been	made	by Mike.
~~Dinner~~		~~will have been being~~	~~made~~	~~by Mike.~~
Dinner	*Future Progresive*	is going to be	made	by Mike
	Future (is going tobe)			

Exercise 8.1

Change the following sentences from active to passive.

1. Michael is eating the pizza.

   The pizza is being eaten by Michael.

2. Kim washed the tablecloth.

   The tablecloth was washed by Kim.

3. Dad will make dinner.

   Dinner will be made by Dad.

4. Mom set the table.

   The table was set by mom.

5. Van did the dishes.

   The dishes was done by Van.

6. Sidia put the dishes away.

   The dishes was put away by Sidia.

7. My brother will bake the cake.

   The cake will be baked by my brother.

8. The birthday boy will blow out the candles.

   The candles will be blowed out by the birthday boy.

9. Susan brought napkins.

   Napkins were brought by Susan.

10. Joe will sing happy birthday.

    Happy birthday will be (sing) by Joe

11. Margret signed the birthday card.

    The birthday card was signed by Margret.

12. John was reading the birthday card.

    The birthday card was being read by John.

13. He will have thanked the guests by the time they leave.

    The guests will be thanked by him by time they leave.

14. He decorated the cake.

    The cake was decorated by him.

15. She gave him a kiss.

    He was given a kiss by her.

Not all active sentences can be changed to passive. As shown above, a sentence needs a subject, transitive verb, which take an object, and an object in order to be changed to passive. Remember that the object of the active sentence becomes the subject of the passive, and the subject of the active sentence becomes part of the "by phrase" at the end of the passive sentence. In order to be able to change a sentence to passive, the question you ask yourself is, "Does the sentence have an object?" If the answer is "yes," you should be able to change it to passive.

It is important to know the difference between an object and a complement, for an object of an active sentence can become the subject of the passive form of that sentence, but the complement of an active sentence cannot be the subject of the passive.

   (a) Someone founded the school in 1965.
   (b) John is intelligent.
   (c) John went to that school.

Sentence (a) has a subject, verb, and an object. The object takes the action from the verb. In other words, if the founding of the school didn't occur, there wouldn't be a school. Simply put: no founding, no school. In sentence (b), we have a subject, verb, and a complement. The word intelligent refers back to John, the subject; the verb is simply linking the subject to the adjective, intelligent. This sentence, therefore, cannot be changed to the passive voice. Similarly, sentence (c) cannot be changed to passive because the complement, "to that school" is a prepositional phrase, and it doesn't take action from the verb. Whether John went to that school or not, the school still exists. However, if someone didn't found the school, the school wouldn't exist.

Exercise 8.2

Change the following sentences to passive if possible.

1. My brother visited me.
   I was visited by my brother

2. My sister came to visit me.

3. She surprised me.
   I was surprised by her.

4. I was surprised.

5. She stayed with me.
   I was stayed with she.

6. She took a lot of pictures during her visit.
   She was taken a lot of pictures during her visit.

7. Joe drinks coffee.
   Joe was drunk coffee.

8. Jonathan drinks heavily.
   Jonathan was drunk heavily.

9. Robert plans his trips.
   Trips were planned by Robert.

10. He plans to go on the trip.
    The trip was planned to go by him.

11. The trip was long.

_____

12. He postponed the trip until next month.

The trip has been postponed until nextmonth by him.

13. He went to the Lincoln Memorial.

_____

14. He visited the Statue of Liberty.

The Statue of Liberty was visited by him.

15. He had a good time.

_____

The "By Phrase"

A sentence is usually in the passive voice if it has or can take a "by phrase." For example, it is easier to tell that the sentence "The child was picked up by her mother," is in the passive voice because of the "by phrase." The sentence "The roads were salted," however, doesn't have a "by phrase" but if the phrase, "by the department of transportation" is added, it becomes obvious that it is in the passive voice.

The use of the "by phrase" may not be necessary if it doesn't provide new, important information. Native speakers do not usually include the "by phrase" in a passive sentence if the "doer" is either not known or is common knowledge. Take for example the sentence, "Someone stole Mary's wallet." The important pieces of information are the disappearance of an item that belongs to Mary, and that the missing item happens to be her wallet. We also know that the wallet can't walk away by itself, but we don't know who stole it. The sentence may, therefore, be stated in the passive as: "Mary's wallet was stolen." In this case, the "by phrase" is not included in the sentence because the "doer" is not known.

Exercise 8.3

_____

Change the following sentences from active to passive. Include the "by phrase" if it provides important information.

1. Something covered my car with snow.

_____

2. Someone removed the snow.

_____

3. My wife shoveled the walkway.

_____

4. Someone took the shovel from the front porch.

_____

5. My neighbor shoveled my driveway.

_____

6. The local authorities lifted the snow emergencies.

_____

7. The police officer gave my sister a speeding ticket.

_____

8. Robert gives me a ride to school every day.

_____

9. Someone enforces the HOV during rush hour.

_____

10. Some concerned citizens raised the issue.

_____

11. Someone sings the national anthem before all star games.

_____

12. Our team won the game.

_____

13. The fans cheer the players throughout the game.

_____

14. My dad will take me to the game.

_____

15. Someone will show the game on television.

_____

Participial Adjectives

A structure that resembles the passive voice is the past participial adjective, for it usually has a form of "be" followed by the past participle as in: He is interested. In this case, the word, interested, is a participial adjective. A related structure is the present participial adjective; however, it does not resemble the passive voice because the participial adjective is in the progressive form. An example of this structure is: "He is interesting."

Certain verbs are used with the suffixes -**ing** and -**ed** to form present and past participial adjectives respectively. However, the two adjectives have different functions. The former causes feeling whereas the latter expresses feeling. For example, the sentence "The students are bored" expresses how the students feel. It is important to note that the past participial adjectives can only be used in reference to people or animals with feeling. However, because people, animals, places, objects, and natural phenomena can cause feelings, the present participial adjective can be used in reference to all of the above.

Exercise 8.4

Determine whether the participial adjective is used correctly.

1. The students are boring. *was bored.*
2. The class is bored. *was boring.*
3. The classroom is boring. *was*
4. The lecture is exciting.
5. The topic is interested. *Interesting*
6. English grammar is amazing.
7. Thunder is frightening.
8. Teaching is exhausting.
9. My notes are confused. *Confusing*
10. I am confusing. *ed*
11. Studying grammar is tiring.
12. Not understanding people can be frustrating.
13. I am frustrating. *ted*
14. She is frustrated. ✓
15. The novel is boring. ✓
16. The writer is boring. *ed*
17. It is humiliating. ✓
18. The actors are inspiring. *ed*
19. The audience is bored. ✓
20. The dancers are thrilled. ✓

Exercise 8.5

Fill in the blanks with an appropriate participial adjective form of the verbs in parenthesis. In some cases both are possible; in such cases, give both participial adjectives.

1. The man is _frightened_ (frighten).

2. The student sitting next to me seemed _interested_ (interest) in grammar.

3. Some people thought the activity was _thrilling_ (thrill).

4. I was not _amused_ (amuse).

5. To say the least, I was _disappointed_ (disappoint).

6. I felt _exhausted_ (exhaust) after the exercise.

7. I was _bored_ (bore).

8. It was _boring_ (bore).

9. Sitting through that lecture was _frustrating_ (frustrate).

10. It was _surprising_ (surprise) to see so many people.

UNIT NINE
Argumentation

OBJECTIVES

By the end of this unit, you should be able:

- ▪ to explain an issue with which you are familiar

- ▪ to construct a sentence that expresses your stance on an issue

- ▪ to state ideas in support of a stance

- ▪ to use techniques to clarify or substantiate reasons including explanation, examples, definition, and reasoning

- ▪ to refute an opposing point of view on an issue with which you are familiar

- ▪ to use subordinators to form adverb clauses

- ▪ to identify sentence types: simple, compound, complex, and compound complex

- ▪ to compose and edit a rough draft of an argumentative paragraph

---

PART I: THE ARGUMENTATIVE PARAGRAPH

Are you an only child? If not, you probably have had an argument with a sibling. An argument between brothers and/or sisters may be in the form of sibling rivalry. Have you ever been involved in sibling rivalry? Sometimes, siblings argue about who is mom or dad's favorite child, whether or not one child has the larger portion at the dinner table, or who has the best birthday present. Such arguments between children are trivial and often end in exchanges such as: Yes, I am; No, you are not, or Yes, I do; No, you don't. Have you had such arguments with a sibling?

When children become adults, they don't stop arguing. Adults form opinions about issues that confront them in life. Some of these issues can be controversial; thus people may have different viewpoints. The ability to argue becomes even more important as you face numerous controversial issues about which you wish to not only take a stand but also show your opponents that your opinion is the right one or a better one.

These days, there are many controversial issues. You may make an assertion on a particular issue based on personal experience, cultural background, religious persuasion, or acquired knowledge. Argument as a system of paragraph development is as important as the other modes of paragraph development you have studied so far.

In this unit, you will work on writing an argumentative paragraph. Unlike the example paragraph where the writer expresses an opinion and provides support, an argumentative paragraph requires many more steps including explanation of the issue, taking a stand, stating your reasons for your assertion, and refuting your opponent's point of view, which may be valid.

Activity 9.1

Paragraph Analysis

Below are two argumentation paragraphs. Read each paragraph carefully and answer the questions that follow.

Paragraph A

Racial profiling is the use of characteristics of a given race in determining who to stop and search because the profiler believes that individuals of the race in question are more likely to commit a crime. Some people argue that it is necessary and others believe that it is a violation of people's rights. I take issue with racial profiling. First of all, in racial profiling, a person is presumed guilty until proven innocent, which is contrary to the notion that a person is innocent until proven guilty. After all, in racial profiling, the only reason an individual of the targeted race is a suspect is because of who he is and not what he has done. Many law-abiding citizens are unduly stopped and searched. A person who commits a crime may be overlooked because he is not of the same race. Secondly, in racial profiling, people are apprehended because they happen to be of the same race as some criminals. I agree that profiling is based on characteristics of people who have committed crimes in the past; however, not every member of a particular race is a criminal. I have no qualms about using behavioral characteristics or even physical characteristics that have been put forth by an eyewitness, but it is totally wrong to concentrate on a group simply because of their racial identity.

Paragraph analysis

1. What is the issue?
2. Does the paragraph include an explanation of the issue?
3. Is the writer for or against racial profiling?
4. What sentence states the writer's stance?
5. Is the writer's stance strong or conditional?
6. How many reasons does the writer give in support of his argument?
7. Does the writer acknowledge his opponent's point of view?
8. How does the writer refute his opponent's point of view?

Paragraph B

Racial profiling is the use of characteristics of a given race in determining who to stop and search because the profiler believes that individuals of the race in question are more likely to commit a crime. Some people say it is necessary; others believe it a violation of civil liberties. I don't think racial profiling is a bad idea. In a heterogeneous society, a society with people of many races, we can't avoid using racial characteristics in an attempt to apprehend people who commit crimes. Law enforcement agents who practice racial profiling use characteristics associated with people of a given race who were involved in previous crimes. I agree that innocent members of the same race may be stopped and searched, but the authorities let them go as soon as they realize that the people they stopped are innocent.

Paragraph analysis

1. What is the issue?
2. Does the paragraph include an explanation of the issue?
3. Is the writer for or against racial profiling?
4. What sentence states the writer's stance?
5. Is the writer's stance strong or conditional?
6. How many reasons does the writer give in support of his argument?
7. Does the writer acknowledge his opponent's point of view?
8. How does the writer refute his opponent's point of view?

Discussion Questions

1. Which of the two paragraphs do you think addresses the issues the best?

2. Which paragraph would you say is closer to the way you feel about the issue?

PART II: ELEMENTS OF AN ARGUMENTATIVE PARAGRAPH

Activity 9.2

Stating the Issue

TASK One of the steps in writing an argumentative paragraph includes stating the issue. In other words, the writer has to show the reader what the contention is. Briefly describe one issue from each of the places given below. In making such a statement, you are answering the question, "What is the issue?"

Example

The United States

Controversy: Racial profiling

What is the issue?

Racial profiling is the use of characteristics of a certain race in determining who to stop and search because the profiler believes that individuals with the same characteristics are more likely to commit a crime. Some people argue that it is necessary and others believe that it is a violation of people's rights.

1. The family

Controversy: _____

What is the issue?

_____

_____

_____

_____

_____

_____

_____

_____

_____

_____

2. Your neighborhood

Controversy: _____

What is the issue?

_____

_____

_____

_____

_____

_____

_____

3. Your county

Controversy: _____

What is the issue?

_____

_____

_____

_____

_____

_____

_____

4. Your state

Controversy: _____

What is the issue?

_____

_____

_____

_____

_____

_____

_____

5. The United States

Controversy: _____

What is the issue?

_____

_____

_____

_____

_____

_____

_____

6. Your country of origin

Controversy: _____

What is the issue?

_____

_____

_____

_____

_____

_____

_____

7. Worldwide

Controversy: _____

What is the issue?

_____

_____

_____

_____

_____

_____

_____

8. Issues across cultures

    Controversy: _____

    What is the issue?

    _____

    _____

    _____

    _____

    _____

    _____

    _____

Activity 9.3

Taking a Stand

In an argumentative paragraph, it is necessary that you take a stand. In other words, you have to let it be known on what side of the argument you are. There are many sentence patterns that can be used to make a sentence that expresses your stance on an issue. Below are patterns that are commonly used.

TASK 1 Carefully study the patterns; pay attention to sentence structure, verbs, and prepositions.

Sentence patterns and sample sentences

1. Subject + verb + the issue
    I support racial profiling.

2. Subject + verb + clause including the issue
    I **believe** female circumcision is unnecessary.
    Other verbs in this category: **Think**
                                        Suppose

3. Subject + verb + preposition + the issue
    I **believe in** racial profiling
    Other verb phrases in this category: **Agree with**
                                               Be for
                                               Be against

4. Subject + verb + noun + preposition + the issue
   I **take issue with** gun control.
   Other verb phrase in this category: **Have qualms about**

5. Subject + verb + preposition + noun + preposition + the issue
   I **am in favor of** the proposed tax hike.
   Other verb phrases in this category: **Be in agreement with**
                                            Be in support of

Error Analysis

TASK 2 Read the following sentences and correct all the mistakes you can find.

1. I am agree with trans-racial adoption.

2. I favor of racial profiling.

3. I against the proposed tax increase.

4. He is disagree with busing.

5. She is in support tuition increase.

6. I for the building of a prison.

7. I am in favor gun control.

8. She against abortion.

9. I am for right to carry concealed weapons.

10. I totally disagree same sex marriage.

11. I have no qualms same sex marriage.

Activity 9.4

Analyzing Sentences That Express a Stance

TASK 1 The sentences below express stances on various issues. Carefully read each sentence and answer the questions that follow.

1. Without a doubt I am in favor of racial profiling.
   Does the statement indicate pro or con?
   Which word or phrase indicates the writer's stance?
   Is the stance strong or weak?
   Is the stance conditional?

2. I have no qualms about eating out every weekend.
   Does the statement indicate pro or con?
   Which word or phrase indicates the writer's stance?
   Is the stance strong or weak?
   Is the stance conditional?

3. I am not in support of a tax increase.
   Does the statement indicate pro or con?
   Which word or phrase indicates the writer's stance?
   Is the stance strong or weak?
   Is the stance conditional?

4. I am for gun control.
   Does the statement indicate pro or con?
   Which word or phrase indicates the writer's stance?
   Is the stance strong or weak?
   Is the stance conditional?

5. I support busing if the neighborhood schools are crowded.
   Does the statement indicate pro or con?
   Which word or phrase indicates the writer's stance?
   Is the stance strong or weak?
   Is the stance conditional?

6. I take issue with female circumcision.
   Does the statement indicate pro or con?
   Which word or phrase indicates the writer's stance?
   Is the stance strong or weak?
   Is the stance conditional?

7. I am totally against the building of this highway.
   Does the statement indicate pro or con?
   Which word or phrase indicates the writer's stance?
   Is the stance strong or weak?
   Is the stance conditional?

8. I am in total disagreement with trans-racial adoption.
   Does the statement indicate pro or con?
   Which word or phrase indicates the writer's stance?
   Is the stance strong or weak?
   Is the stance conditional?

9. I am not in favor of cross-cousin marriages for medical reasons.
   Does the statement indicate pro or con?
   Which word or phrase indicates the writer's stance?
   Is the stance strong or weak?
   Is the stance conditional?

10. I believe racial profiling is an unjust practice.
    Does the statement indicate pro or con?
    Which word or phrase indicates the writer's stance?
    Is the stance strong or weak?
    Is the stance conditional?

TASK 2 Write a sentence indicating your stance on each of the following issues. Make sure that your sentences express your true feeling. In other words, are you strongly or somewhat for or against the issue? If your stance is conditional, your sentence must show that.

1. Gun control

   _____

   _____

2. The death penalty

   _____

   _____

3. Same sex marriage

   _____

   _____

4. Busing

_____

_____

5. Restriction of immigration

_____

_____

6. Raising the tuition at your school

_____

_____

7. Abortion

_____

_____

8. Cross-cousin marriage

_____

_____

9. Trans-racial adoption

_____

_____

10. Racial profiling

_____

_____

Activity 9.5

Giving Reasons for and Against Your Stance

In writing an argumentative paragraph, it is important to have good reasons for your argument as well as knowing the reasons your opponents may use in support of their argument. Before you write a draft of your paragraph, you should think of reasons for and against. The following are some reasons for and against specific issues.

TASK   Add more reasons to those in the columns below.

Issue: Racial profiling

For	**Against**
Helps focus on characteristics observed from previous crimes	All people of the target race should not be judged based on the behavior of a few.
	All members of the target race are presumed guilty until proven innocent.
_____	_____
_____	_____
_____	_____
_____	_____
_____	_____

Issue: The death penalty

For

Only used for those who take
other people's lives; punishment fits
the crime

_____

_____

_____

_____

_____

_____

Against

It does not deter crime

_____

_____

_____

_____

_____

_____

Issue: Senior citizens over 80 should be licensed to drive

For

They do not have to depend on others.

They only drive when it is absolutely
necessary

_____

_____

_____

_____

_____

Against

They are slow to react in emergencies.

They have poor eyesight.

_____

_____

_____

_____

_____

Activity 9.6

Supporting Ideas

When writing an argumentative paragraph, it may not be enough to simply state a reason for your opinion. You may have to explain your reason, define terms you use in your paragraph that your readers may not know, give examples, show causal relationships or give statistics to convince your opponent. Remember, the main purpose of an argument is to convince your opponents to accept your point of view, so you have to give enough good reasons to convince them.

TASK The following are examples of techniques you can use to clarify or substantiate your reasons. Study them carefully. Remember that you don't have to use all of them. For example, you may not have statistics in support of an argument; however, you can narrate an anecdote to show an actual occurrence as evidence.

Issue: Racial profiling

Statement: Profiling helps focus on characteristics observed from previous crimes.

Explanation: In other words, if a large number of people with certain characteristics commit a crime, it makes sense to concentrate on those characteristics in an attempt to apprehend likely offenders.

Reasoning:

Issue: Dumping hazardous waste

Term: Nimby

Reasoning: Some chemicals cause cancer. The hazardous waste has chemicals. If it is dumped in our neighborhood, we may develop cancer.

Definition: Nimby is an acronym that spells out—not in my backyard; people usually do not oppose an issue unless it directly has an impact on them.

Issue: Racial profiling

Example of problems with racial profiling

Examples: For example, profile of the person who would most likely perpetrate the sniper incidents in the D.C. area turned out to be inaccurate.

Issue: Tuition increase

Statistics: The tuition was increased by only 1%

Activity 9.7

Refutation

In a reasonable argument, you must put the opposing points of view into consideration. Even though it is very important to present enough sound reasons in a logical way in support of your stance, it is essential to show that you are aware of the valid points given by the other side. Nevertheless, you have to show the shortcomings of the opposing argument. More importantly, show that you have better reasons and/or that your reasons are more logical. This is done in the form of refutation, to show that the evidence of the opposing argument is incorrect, insufficient, or illogical.

TASK 1   If you know that your opponent is wrong, you must point out the inaccuracies. Below are examples of sentences that express opinion about flawed arguments. Circle the word or phrase that signifies inaccuracy in each sentence, and underline the given inaccurate information.

1.   My opponent is wrong; the rate of unemployment is above 5 percent.

2.   My opponent is incorrect; blacks are no longer the largest minority group in the United States.

3.   My opponent is mistaken. Arranged marriages do not always end in divorce. As a matter of fact, there are more divorces in the U.S., where arranged marriages are non-existent than in my country, where arranged marriage is the tradition.

4.   My opponent's argument is false. The death penalty does not deter crime.

5. My opponent's argument is untrue. All the members of the target culture are not presumed guilty until proven innocent. Only a handful is apprehended once in a while.

6. My opponent's reasons are erroneous. Senior citizens do not drive only when it is necessary. Some of them go for a spin every now and then.

7. My opponent's reasoning is faulty. Not all waste has chemicals; only hazardous waste may have chemicals that cause cancer. The waste in that dump, although malodorous, does not cause cancer.

8. My opponent's reasons are wide of the mark. A matchmaker is not necessarily a member of the extended family of either the bride or the groom.

Another form of refutation is to admit that your opponent has a valid point, but show that it has short-comings and that your reason is a lot stronger. For example, someone may put forth the argument that a child with adoptive parents of a different race may be confused about his identity. However, it may be argued that a child in a foster home without parents will be even more confused. This type of rebuttal is often in the form of a compound sentence with a connector of concession.

TASK 2 Read the sample sentences below and underline the contrast concession words and phrases.

1. I agree with your point that a child of adoptive parents may be confused about his identity; nevertheless, I strongly believe that a child living in a foster home without a set of parents will be even more confused.

2. I agree that adults have a right to smoke if they wish; however, they have no right to make me inhale secondhand smoke.

3. Even though female circumcision has been a tradition in some societies, the risks associated with the practice outweigh the benefits.

4. Despite the fact that schools in our neighborhood are excellent, they are crowded, so I think children should be bused to other neighborhood schools.

PART III: WRITING YOUR ARGUMENTATIVE PARAGRAPH

Activity 9.8

Generating Ideas

Controversial Issues

There are many controversial issues in the world today. Some contentious issues come up in families, neighborhoods, counties, states, countries or even the world as whole. One issue that came up in Northern Virginia, for example, was the idea of having a professional baseball team. The state of Virginia does not have a professional sports team, be it baseball, basketball, football, or hockey. The issue became a bone of contention in Arlington County when the proponents of baseball in Northern Virginia proposed that a stadium be built in the county. Some people who cried out against the idea claimed that the time and money spent on building a stadium could be used on other pressing needs such as affordable housing. Those who are against building the stadium also claim that traffic in the county will get worse if a stadium is built. Proponents argue that baseball in Northern Virginia would bring jobs and revenue to the county. The controversy is in evidence in the county. Signs in support of both sides of the issue can be seen on lawns throughout the county. In one neighborhood, two next door neighbors on opposing sides of the issue have signs in their front yard proudly displaying their sentiment on the controversy.

TASK 1 Can you think of controversial issues in each of the following places listed below? Add other issues you come up with to the items listed.

1. Your family or families in general
    Doing chores around the house
    Spending money

    _____

    _____

    _____

2. Your neighborhood

    _____

    _____

    _____

    _____

    _____

    _____

3. County
   Busing children to and from school
   Snow removal

   _____

   _____

   _____

4. State
   Tax increases
   Building new roads
   The death penalty

   _____

   _____

   _____

5. The United States
   Gun control
   Trans-racial adoption
   Racial profiling

   _____

   _____

   _____

6. Your country of origin

   _____

   _____

   _____

   _____

   _____

7. Worldwide issues
   Immigration
   Trade
   Same sex marriage

   _____

   _____

   _____

8. Other issues are controversial across cultures. Some practices that were the norm in certain cultures have become controversial. For example, certain initiation rites that have been practiced for generations in some cultures may be deemed unnecessary and even harmful. Those who argue for the continuation of such practices may base their argument on tradition whereas the opponents may base their argument on scientific knowledge or human rights. The following are controversial issues across cultures. Can you add others from your culture?

Female circumcision
Arranged marriages
Marrying a cross-cousin (a man marrying his father's sister's daughter or his mother's brother's daughter)

_____

_____

_____

TASK 2 Discuss, in groups or as a class, the controversial issues across cultures that students came up with. Make sure that you understand the issues. If you are not sure about an issue, ask the teacher or other students to clarify it or give you examples.

Activity 9.9

Vocabulary Used in Argumentation

TASK 1 The following words are often used in arguments. Look up their meanings and other related forms such as adjective, verb, and adverb.

Issue

Controversy

Contention

Argument

Debate

Disagreement

TASK 2 Use each word or a related form and the given issue in a sentence. Remember, an issue is not necessarily controversial. For example, the building of a highway may be an issue in a community, but the location of the highway may be controversial because people may not want it in their backyard, the NIMBY (not in my back yard) phenomenon.

Example

Controversy / trans-racial adoption

Sentence: Trans-racial adoption is controversial in the United States.

1. Contention / the proposed tax increase

   Sentence: _____

   _____

2. Debate / the effectiveness of racial profiling

   Sentence: _____

   _____

3. Argument / whether the highway should go through the neighborhood

   Sentence: _____

   _____

4. Controversy / arranged marriage

   Sentence: _____

   _____

5. Disagreement / building a stadium in the county

   Sentence: _____

   _____

6. Issue / whether senior citizens over 80 should drive

   Sentence: _____

   _____

Writing Assignment

Write a paragraph in which you argue for or against trans-racial adoption. Make sure that your paragraph includes a clear explanation of the issue and your stance. Also remember to give reasons for your argument as well as refute opposing points of view.

PART IV: ENABLING GRAMMAR EXERCISES

Adverb Clauses

Subordinate or dependent clauses are used with independent clauses to form complex sentences. A subordinate clause may be an adverb clause of time cause, manner, reason, condition, result, purpose, place, or contrast. Study the subordinating conjunctions and the sample sentences below. Pay attention to punctuation.

Examples

(a) Time

Immediate:

As soon as   **As soon as** I got home, I called her.

Sequence:

Before   I called her **before** I left the house.

After   I had breakfast **after** I took a shower.

Co-occurrence:

While   I was reading the paper **while** I was eating breakfast.

At the time (of):

When   **When** he called, I was taking a shower.

As   **As** I was leaving the store, it started to rain

(b) Reason

Because   **Because** I am new in this state, I have to pay out of state tuition.

Since   **Since** I don't have a car, I have to take the bus to school.

(c) Result

So...that   The test was **so** hard **that** everyone failed.

Such...that   It was **such** a hard test **that** everyone failed it.

(d) Manner

As if   He was looking at me **as if** he didn't believe me.

(e) Condition

If   I don't have to drive **if** you can give me a ride.

Provided that   I will be there **provided that** I am able to take off from work.

On condition that   I will stay with the company **on condition that** I get a raise.

(f) Purpose

So that   I studied hard **so that** I could raise my GPA.

For the purpose of   I studied hard **for the** sole **purpose** of raising my GPA.

(g) Place

Where   I like to sit **where** I can see everyone who enters the room.

Wherever   Please take me with you **wherever** you go.

(h) Contrast concession

Even though   **Even though** I studied for the test, I failed it.

Although   **Although** I am full, I can eat another slice of pizza.

Though   **Though** I was exhausted, I stayed to watch the movie.

Despite the fact that **Despite the fact that** I was tired, I stayed up to watch the movie.

In spite of the act that I like living in Canada **in spite of the fact that** it gets cold.

In spite of   I like Alaska **in spite of** the cold.

(i) Comparison

More ...than   I ate **more** pizza **than** you did.

More than   I ate **more than** you did.

As...as   He is **as** tall **as** his brother.

Exercise 9.1

Determine the relationship between the sentences in each pair and combine them using the appropriate subordinator.

1. It started to rain.
   I opened my umbrella.

   _____

   _____

2. I had an umbrella.
   I got wet.

   _____

   _____

3. Classes were canceled.
   We had three feet of snow.

   _____

   _____

4. It was raining.
   I was waiting for the bus.

   _____

   _____

5. It was raining hard.
   My windshield wipers could not wipe off the water fast enough.

   _____

   _____

6. He is tall.
   His brother is taller.

   _____

   _____

7. He ate.
   I ate more.

   _____

   _____

8. It was a big piece.
I couldn't finish it.

_____

_____

9. Invite me.
I will come to your birthday party.

_____

_____

10. He was born in China.
He doesn't speak Chinese.

_____

_____

11. They are twins.
They don't look alike.

_____

_____

Sentence Types

The sentence types most often used in writing are: simple, compound, complex, and compound complex. A simple sentence is an independent clause that expresses a complete idea. The simple sentence usually has a subject, a verb, and expresses a complete thought. A complex sentence has one independent clause and at least one dependent clause. A compound sentence has two or more independent clauses, and a compound complex sentence has at least two independent clauses and at least one dependent clause.

When writing, a phrase can be used as part of a sentence, but it doesn't express a complete thought, nor does it change the sentence type. A dependent clause does not express a complete thought either; however, when used in a sentence, it can change the sentence type.

Examples

Dialing a rotary phone and dialing a cellular phone. (Phrase)

If he picks up the receiver and dials the number. (Dependent clause)

The cellular phone is portable. (Independent clause / Simple sentence)

Because he has a cellular phone, he can call anytime. (Complex sentence)

You can store numbers on a cellular phone, but you can't do that on a rotary phone. (Compound sentence)

He took your number, and he took his cellular phone so that he could call you from the airport. (Compound complex)

Exercise 9.2

State whether each of the following is a phrase, a dependent clause, or an independent clause.

1. _____ Dialing a number on a rotary phone.

2. _____ Why are cellular phone users?

3. _____ The convenience of owning a cellular phone.

4. _____ The cost of using a cellular phone.

5. _____ When I was in my country.

6. _____ That he has a cellular phone.

7. _____ Take your cellular phone.

8. _____ Rotary phones are now relics.

9. _____ Cellular phones come in handy.

10. _____ Be nice to him when you call.

11. _____ In order to make a call on a rotary phone.

12. _____ You must not make that call.

13. _____ He has a good cellular phone.

14. _____ Why do you think he has a cellular phone?

Exercise 9.3

Identify the following combinations of phrases, dependent clauses and independent clauses by putting the sentence type or fragment, i.e., incomplete sentence on the line provided. The first two have been done for you.

1. (_____Complex_____) Ind. Clause + Dep. Clause

2. (_____Fragment_____) Dep. Clause

3. (_____) Ind. Clause + Ind. Clause

4. (_____) Phrase + Ind. Clause

5. (_____) Dep. Clause + Ind. Clause

6. (_____) Ind. Clause + Ind. Clause + Dep. Clause

7. (_____) Phrase + Ind. Clause + Dep. Clause

8. (_____) Ind. Clause

9. (_____) Dep. Clause + Dep. Clause

10. (_____) Phrase

11. (_____) Dep. Clause + Ind. Clause + Phrase

12. (_____) Ind. Clause + Ind. Clause + Ind. Clause

13. (_____) Ind. Clause + Phrase + Dep. Clause

14. (_____) Phrase + Ind. Clause + Ind. Clause

15. (_____) Phrase + Dep. Clause

Exercise 9.4

Punctuate the following sentences if necessary.

1. She bought me a beautiful shirt however I brought it back for it was too small.

2. The stores were crowded nevertheless I went shopping for it was the last day before Christmas.

3. Not only was I a good baseball player but I was also a good basketball player.

4. He plays both baseball and basketball.

5. Neither my brother nor my sister went to the game.

6. We will either go to the game or watch it on television.

7. Both the baseball game and the hockey game were televised.

8. I bought a ticket however I did not go to the hockey game.

9. Our team played very well nevertheless we lost.

10. Neither our team nor their team was capable of scoring a goal.

UNIT TEN
Introduction to the Essay

OBJECTIVES

By the end of this unit, you should be able:

- ■ to distinguish between elements of a paragraph and elements of an essay
- ■ to distinguish between a topic sentence and a thesis statement
- ■ to state the differences between developing ideas introduced in a topic sentence and developing ideas introduced in a thesis statement
- ■ to state differences between a concluding sentence and a concluding paragraph
- ■ to distinguish between sentence connectors and paragraph connectors

---

PART I: PARAGRAPHS AND ESSAYS: SIMILARITIES AND DIFFERENCES

In units one through nine, you worked on writing paragraphs. You have written paragraphs of different rhetorical modes. For example, you may have written a paragraph developed by examples, in which you had an idea or opinion expressed in your topic sentence and gave reasons or examples to support it. Other paragraphs you have written include cause and effect, comparison and contrast, and argumentation. Up to this point, you have been writing paragraphs that focus on one idea with support sentences and a conclusion.

In this unit, you will work on writing essays. An essay is similar to a paragraph in that both pieces of writing introduce an idea or ideas at the beginning, provide support in the body, and have a conclusion at the end of the piece. The two, however, have more differences as shown in the table that follows. For instance, the main idea of a paragraph is the topic sentence, whereas the main idea of an essay is the thesis statement. A paragraph is usually about one idea, and an essay discusses two or more ideas; as a result, an essay is much longer than a paragraph.

Another difference has to do with content. A paragraph has a topic sentence, support sentences, and a concluding sentence. On the other hand, an essay has an introductory paragraph with an attention getter and a thesis statement, body paragraphs that develop the ideas stated in the thesis statement, and a concluding paragraph. As you can see, there are similarities as well as differences between a paragraph and an essay.

The table that follows lists the differences between a paragraph and an essay. Familiarize yourself with the differences and pay attention to the characteristics of an essay as outlined in the right column.

Paragraph	Essay
Single paragraph	Multiple paragraphs
One indentation	Multiple indentations
Topic sentence	Thesis statement
A paragraph develops one idea stated in the topic sentence	An essay develops ideas stated in the thesis statement
May not have an attention getter	Usually has an attention getter
Main idea usually given in the first sentence	Main idea usually given in the last sentence of the introductory paragraph
Has a concluding sentence	Has a concluding paragraph
Does not need transition words between paragraphs	Needs transition words between paragraphs

PART II: THE ESSAY

Just as paragraphs can be in various rhetorical modes, so can essays. However, the focus in this introduction to writing essays will be on the example essay.

An essay comprises of three main parts: introduction, body, and conclusion. The introduction has an attention grabber and a thesis statement. It is important for a writer to get the attention of a reader and maintain it. To do this, you should think of strategies that may get a reader's attention. These may include general statements about the topic that may be of interest to a reader. These statements can be answers to who, what, when, where, and how questions about the topic. For example, when writing an essay about a friend, you may begin by saying who he is, what he does, when you met, where you met, and how long you have known each other. This background information leads the reader to the specific ideas stated in the thesis statement.

Another attention getter is an anecdote. A short story at the beginning of an essay may not only get the reader's attention but also make the reader interested in what comes next. Other attention grabbers are statistics and quotations, particularly from well-known authorities.

After getting the readers' attention, you should state the ideas you want them to know about the topic. These ideas are given in the thesis statement—the main ideas of the essay. The thesis statement often comes at the end of the introductory paragraph and after the attention grabber.

Next in the essay are the body paragraphs. The number of body paragraphs depends on the number of ideas in your thesis statement. For instance, if there are three ideas in your thesis statement, there should be at least three body paragraphs—one for each idea.

The paragraphs you have written, ranging from the example paragraph in unit one to argumentation in unit nine, are in body paragraph format. In other words, a body paragraph has a topic sentence, support sentences, and a concluding sentence. In body paragraphs, you give examples, details, statistics, explanations, definitions, and so on; anything that can be used to support the ideas in your thesis statement.

Last but not least is the conclusion. In this paragraph, you may restate the thesis statement, summarize the ideas given in the body paragraphs, make general comments about the ideas in the body paragraphs, or give a plan of action. You can have a combination of any or all of these in your concluding paragraph. In other words, you may restate the thesis, summarize the ideas in the body paragraphs, and state a plan of action in your conclusion.

The conclusion you choose may depend on the type of essay you write. For instance, in a process essay, you may state the result of the process, whereas in a cause and effect essay, you may discuss what has to be done to maintain the effect if it is a positive outcome or avoid it if it is a negative outcome. A concluding paragraph on obesity, for example, may have information on what one has to do to avoid being obese. However, a concluding paragraph on the causes of good health may have advice on how to have or maintain good health.

Activity 10.1

Essay Analysis

TASK   Read the following essay and answer the questions that follow.

When I tell people I don't have a cellular phone, they look at me as if I am an alien that landed on earth from another planet. These perplexed individuals can't believe that I can exist on earth without a cell phone. "Why don't you have a cell phone?" is a question I am often asked. Those who pose such a question can't think of a reason why anyone would choose to live without one. A friend even asked me if there is a religious or moral reason for not owning a cell phone. "Absolutely not," I said. Even though I don't have one, I must admit that the cell is a useful modern device. Unlike its predecessor, the landline, the cellular phone is not only used for communicating with others, but also for getting information and for entertainment.

One use of the cell phone is to communicate with others from afar. Using a cell phone, one can call and have a conversation with anyone who has a phone, just by dialing his or her number. With a cell phone, however, communication can also occur through text messaging. In this case, the sender types the message on the phone and sends it to the receiver. The receiver, in turn, can text a reply right back. In the past, this type of written communication only occurred in the form of a letter, and it took a while to write a letter, mail it, and get a reply, but nowadays, with a cell phone, it is possible to communicate with others at anytime and anywhere. In addition to calling and text messaging, one can send photos. As you can see, with a cell phone, not only can you communicate with others, but they can see what you look like.

Another use of the cell phone is for getting information. In this day and age, people are in need of a lot of information to carry on with their lives. For example, to start the day, it may be necessary to get the weather forecast, so with the touch of button, one can find out whether it is going to rain so as to take an umbrella to work or get the temperature forecast in order to dress appropriately. Furthermore, people who invest in the stock market have to know what happened in the market not only in their country but also in other parts of the world, and they can do that with a cell phone. Other pieces of information one can get include the score of a game. One night, for instance, I was watching a football game, but I went to bed before it ended. The next morning, I asked my son what the score was. He immediately took out his cell phone, pushed a few buttons, and told me the score. With a cell phone, it is even possible to have the worldwide web right in your hands.

Yet another use of the cell phone is for entertainment. Cell phones have games that people can use to entertain themselves when stranded at an airport or are alone at home. One game that is commonly played by cell phone owners is solitaire. While alone, an individual can pass the time by playing this card game. Other games include puzzles such as Sudoku and photo puzzles. These games, a number puzzle and a photo puzzle respectively, are on cell phones and can be used to occupy one's free time. Another form of entertainment is listening to music. Cell phone owners can download music of their choice for their listening pleasure at anytime. With a cell phone, people can be entertained wherever they are.

Cell phones are not only used to interact with others, but they can also be used to get information as well as for entertainment. To many people, the cell phone has become indispensable. No wonder, some people believe that these days, anyone who doesn't have a cell phone is the odd man out. I truly believe that in the very near future, the cell phone will be a necessity, and at that time, I will have no choice but to own one to the delight of some of my friends.

1. Does the introduction have an attention grabber?
2. Does the essay have a thesis statement?
3. How many ideas are in the thesis statement?
4. What examples of the use of cell phones are stated?
5. Is there a concluding paragraph?
6. What kind of conclusion does the writer use?
7. Are there paragraph connectors?
8. What kind of essay is this? → Analysis

PART III: ELEMENTS OF THE ESSAY

Activity 10.2

Attention Grabber

Remember that it is necessary to get the attention of your readers from the start. Some strategies that are often used to grab a reader's attention are stated at the beginning of this unit.

TASK   Which of the following do you think can be an attention grabber in an essay with the following thesis statement: John is friendly, intelligent, and has a sense of humor. What kind of attention grabber is it?

    a.   I met John in high school. We became very good friends by the end of that academic year. We have known each other for fifteen years. I like him a lot. He is one of my favorite friends.

    b.   I came to class early the first day because I was a little nervous. I didn't know what to expect. I was the first one to arrive, and as I sat there, a tall, lanky guy walked in. He greeted me and then asked if that was the right class. He seemed very friendly, but I thought that was only because it was the first day of class. I was wrong. John is very friendly.

    c.   John had just registered for the class minutes before. He didn't think he would be able to enroll in the class because the class was full. He was lucky. I registered early. I had nothing to worry about.

Activity 10.3

Thesis Statement

A thesis statement has the subject and two or more ideas about the subject you wish to discuss or support. These ideas are not too general and not too specific. If they are too general, you could write a book on them, and if they are too specific they may not be supportable.

Also, a thesis statement suggests the writer's plan of action. In other words, from the thesis statement, a reader can tell what type of essay is to follow and in what order the ideas are to be discussed in the body paragraphs.

TASK   Which of the following do you think is a good thesis statement? Give reasons for your opinion.

1. I don't like cell phones because they can be dangerous, disruptive, and expensive.
2. My city is a good place to live, work, and play.
3. Our class is interesting but challenging.
4. My parents differ in their attitude toward parenting and outlook on life.
5. Today's teenagers are different in the way they dress, behave, and speak.
6. My brother is tall, affable, and intelligent.
7. Students who take good notes, study hard, and talk to their teacher on a regular basis do well in school.
8. My neighborhood is safe, quiet, and convenient.
9. Speeding, cell phone use, and falling asleep while driving are common causes of traffic accidents.
10. My teacher is tall, slim, and hardworking.

Activity 10.4

Body Paragraphs

Body paragraphs are similar to the paragraphs you have written in units one through nine. A body paragraph has a topic sentence, support sentences, and a concluding sentence. Body paragraphs usually appear in the order the ideas are stated in the thesis statement. For instance, if a thesis statement is as follows: My neighborhood is clean, quiet, and convenient, the first body paragraph will be about the neighborhood being clean, the second will discuss the area being quiet, and the third body paragraph will be about its convenience.

Also make sure that you arrange your paragraphs in such a way that the negative ideas or the positive ideas are together; do not mix them. For example, the thesis statement: My neighborhood is convenient, noisy, and safe, should be: My neighborhood is convenient, safe, but noisy. This way, the two positive ideas are discussed first, and then the negative idea is discussed last. The statement could also be: My neighborhood is noisy but safe and convenient.

Body paragraphs must be connected to show the logical flow of the essay. Connectors of body paragraphs can be divided into four categories: those used to introduce the first body paragraph, which also connect the introductory paragraph to it; ones that begin the second body paragraph; those used to introduce second or subsequent body paragraphs; and the conjunctions that introduce the last body paragraph. The use of correct connectors will create a smooth transition from one paragraph to the next.

TASK 1 Study the following connectors and familiarize yourself with those in each category.

A. **Connectors used to introduce the first body paragraph**
   One thing I like about him is...
   To begin with,

First,
Firstly,
First of all,
The most common cause is...

B. Connectors used to introduce the second body paragraph
Second,
Secondly,

C. Connectors used to introduce the second and/or subsequent body paragraphs
Another reason is...
Next,
Yet another factor is...
Also,

D. Connectors used to introduce the final body paragraph
Yet another example is...
Finally,
Last but not least,

TASK 2 The following are different types of essays and transitions between three body paragraphs of essays of various rhetorical styles. Determine the type of essay for each group of transitions.

Types of essays

Classification
Example
Cause and effect
Comparison and contrast
Argumentation
Extended definition
Description
Process
Narration

Essay type: _____

1. One step is...
    Another step is...
    Yet another step in the process is...

Essay type_____

2. Let's consider the shape of...
    Next are the colors of...
    Last but not least is the texture of...

Essay type_____

3. First, he...
    Then he...
    In the end, he...

    Essay type: _____

4. To begin with...
    Another example...
    Still another example...

    Essay type: _____

5. It is a...
    It is used for...
    It can be also be used for...

    Essay type: _____

6. One reason for...
    Another common cause is...
    The most common cause is...

    Essay type: _____

7. One similarity between them is...
    In like manner, they...
    They are also similar in...

    Essay type: _____

8. One category is...
    The second group is made of...
    Yet another category is...

    Essay type: _____

9. To begin with...
    Another reason I have no qualms about the issue is...
    Most important of all, I ...

Relevance of Support Sentences in Body Paragraphs

The support sentences in a body paragraph must also be relevant. That is to say, they must relate to and, most importantly, support the controlling idea of the topic sentence.

TASK   Read the topic sentence and its support sentences, and determine which of them are relevant. Cross out the support sentences that are irrelevant.

Topic sentence: My roommate is irresponsible.

    a.   He doesn't do his homework on time.

    b.   He has dirty dishes all over the living room.

    c.   He never opens his mail let alone reads it.

    d.   He makes his bed.

    e.   He is a procrastinator.

    f.   He can never get up in the morning.

    g.   He never replies to his parents' letters.

    h.   He never puts away his clothes.

    i.   He leaves the keys to the apartment in the door.

    j.   He often runs out of gas.

    k.   He irons his clothes.

Activity 10.5

Concluding Paragraph

A concluding paragraph is as important as the introductory paragraph. In the introductory paragraph, you try to get the reader's attention and state the ideas you intend to discuss in your essay. In the concluding paragraph, however, you can do a number of things, depending on the type of essay you are writing. In an example essay, for instance, you may choose to restate your thesis statement and summarize the supporting ideas in your body paragraphs. This way the reader is left with a summary of the ideas and a reaffirmation of the thesis statement.

The concluding paragraph of a cause and effect essay may give advice on what can be done to maintain or avoid the effect depending on whether it is positive or negative. For example, in an essay that discusses the causes of an illness, the concluding paragraph would include what has to be done to avoid this undesirable effect.

Other concluding paragraphs can be a comment, plan of action, or a look to the future. Comments are remarks or opinions the writer gives in closing given the ideas discussed in the body paragraphs. A plan of action indicates what the writer wants to do about the issues discussed, whereas a look to the future is a prediction one is making given the thesis statement and the support in the body paragraphs.

PART IV: WRITING YOUR ESSAY

Activity 10.6

Generating Ideas

Before you start writing, try to generate ideas about your topic. There are many ways to gather ideas. One way is to write freely on your topic. This initial piece usually includes useful ideas as well as ideas you may not need to write the first draft of your essay. Another way to generate ideas is to list words or phrases pertaining to the topic. These can then be categorized, and body paragraphs of an essay can be developed by using the ideas in each category.

This stage of essay development is important for a number of reasons. First of all, it allows you to jot down your ideas on paper or on a computer. Secondly, ideas do not usually come in a logically sequenced way that is suitable for academic writing. Ideas tend to come in bits and pieces, and your task as a writer is to put them in complete thoughts and rearrange them to form coherent paragraphs. It is easier to do all these on paper or on a computer than in your mind.

Categorizing Ideas

The following ideas were given by students in a low-intermediate ESL class during a brainstorming exercise about their teacher. As you can see, the ideas are not in logical order. Some of them are about how the teacher looks, others are about his personality, yet others are about his experience.

TASK 1 Put the ideas under the appropriate category.

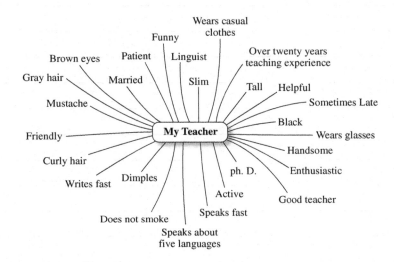

Appearance	Personality	Experience
Tall	Friendly	Over twenty years teaching experience

Forming Sentences with Words or Phrases in Categories

TASK 2 Choose one category and put all the items in that category into complete sentences.

Example: **Appearance**

Tall   My teacher is tall.

_____   _____

_____   _____

_____   _____

_____   _____

_____   _____

_____   _____

_____   _____

_____   _____

_____   _____

Personality

Friendly   My teacher is friendly.

_____   _____

_____   _____

_____   _____

_____   _____

_____   _____

_____   _____

_____   _____

_____   _____

_____   _____

Experience

Over twenty years

Teaching experience: My teacher has over twenty years of teaching experience.

_____

_____

_____

_____

_____

_____

_____

Activity 10.7

Writing a Draft

What you have at the end of the categorization process is a list of complete sentences about the appearance, personality, or experience of this teacher, and the sentences in each category provide the building blocks of a paragraph.

TASK   With these sentences, write a rough draft of an essay on this teacher's appearance, personality, or experience in the space provided.

_____

_____

_____

_____

_____

_____

_____

_____

_____

_____

_____

_____

_____

_____

_____

_____

_____

_____

_____

_____

_____

_____

_____

_____

_____

_____

_____

_____

_____

_____

Activity 10.8

Editing

TASK Use the following questions to edit your essay.

1. Does the introduction have an attention grabber?
2. Does the essay have a thesis statement?
3. Is there a concluding paragraph?
4. What kind of conclusion do you have?
5. Are there paragraph connectors?

PART V: ENABLING GRAMMAR EXERCISES

Causative

A causative sentence has a subject and a causative verb. Those are then followed by a clause that begins with a proper noun, pronoun, or noun phrase that functions as the object of the initial clause even though it is in the subject position of the second clause. In a causative sentence the author makes, lets, or has someone do something, and that something is what is stated in the clause that follows the causative verb. Causative verbs can be divided into two types: verbs that take the base form of the verb in the second clause and those that take the infinitive in the second clause.

Type A: Causative Verbs That Take the Base Form of the Verb in the Second Clause

Subject	Causative verb	Object/Subject	Verb	Object
I	had	my friend	review	my paper
She	let	her brother	do	the dishes
My brother	made	me	eat	his broccoli

The causative verbs provided have different meanings. When the causative verb, *have*, is used, the intended meaning is to want something done by another person. When the verb *make* is used, however, the intended meaning is forcing somebody to do something. Use of the verb *let* denotes giving someone permission to do something he or she wants to do.

1. He let his son go to the game. (His son wanted to go to the game, and he let him go.)

2. He had his friend look over his essay before he turned it in. (He wanted his friend to review the paper before he turned it in.)

3. She made her daughter clean her room. (She forced her daughter to clean her room, a chore which she probably didn't want to do.)

Exercise 10.1

Determine which of the following causative verbs: **have, let, make** is appropriate for each of the following situations, and write a complete sentence using the items provided.

1. You / your neighbor / to park in your designated parking spot

   _____

   _____

2. A police officer / you / to go through a street with barricades

   _____

   _____

3. The lady / her husband / to do the dishes

   _____

   _____

4. Your dad / you / to use the car

   _____

   _____

5. Your mother / you / to come home before the party ended

   _____

   _____

6. Your teacher / you / to leave early

   _____

   _____

7. You / your doctor / to take your temperature

   _____

   _____

8. Your mother / you / stay up late

_____

_____

9. You / your teacher / to write you a recommendation letter

_____

_____

10. Your friend / her daughter / to clean her room

_____

_____

11. You / a man walking his dog / to pick up after him

_____

_____

12. You / your neighbor / to give you a ride to work

_____

_____

13. You / your mechanic / to change the oil

_____

_____

14. The mother / her child / to buy whatever she wants with the money she got for her birthday

_____

_____

15. He / his wife / decide / whether she wants to eat out for her birthday

_____

_____

Type B: Causative Verbs That Take the Infinitive in the Second Clause

Subject	Causative verb	Object/Subject	Verb	Object
I	allowed	my brother	to take	the car
I	permitted	my students	to use	a calculator
My brother	instructed	me	to mow	the lawn

The causative verbs *allow* and *permit* mean letting another person or others do something. The verb, *instruct,* however, means to direct. In other words, when you use the causative verb *instruct,* you are telling the addressee(s) what to do.

1. He instructed his son to go clean his room. (He told his son what to do—that is, clean his room.)

2. He allowed the students to use a calculator during the exam. (He gave the students permission to use a calculator during the exam.)

3. The doctor permitted the patient to go home over the weekend. (The doctor allowed the patient to go home over the weekend.)

Exercise 10.2

Determine which of the following causative verbs: ***allow, permit, instruct*** is appropriate for each of the following situations, and write a complete sentence using the items provided.

1. The teacher / students / use a dictionary to do their in-class writing assignment

   _____

   _____

2. The little girl / her friend / play with her toys

   _____

   _____

3. The travel agent / me / change my itinerary

   _____

   _____

4. The waitress / patron / change his order

_____

_____

5. The police officer / drunk driver / get off the road

_____

_____

6. Our history teacher / us / use our textbook during the test

_____

_____

7. The speaker / the security guard / get the demonstrators out of the building

_____

_____

8. My teacher / me / turn in my late assignment

_____

_____

9. The building supervisor / the tenants / not to leave garbage in hallway

_____

_____

10. The supervisor / the salesperson / give the customer a refund

_____

_____

A causative sentence can be in various tenses. To change the tense of a sentence, all that has to be done is to change the causative verb, which is the main verb of the initial clause. The verb in the second clause, which is either in the base form or infinitive, does not change. See the following examples:

1. I have my friend look over my assignment.
   I had my friend look over my assignment.

2. I always let my sister vacuum our room.
   Yesterday, I let my sister vacuum our room.

3. He makes me clean his room.
   He made me clean his room.

4. Our teacher allows us to use a calculator.
   Our teacher allowed us to use a calculator.

5. She instructs me to do house chores.
   She instructed me to do house chores.

Exercise 10.3

Change each of the following sentences into the tense indicated in brackets.

1. I had the tailor hem my dress.

   (Simple future) _____

   _____

2. My daughter will not let her brother tuck her in.

   (Simple past) _____

   _____

3. He allows us to use a calculator.

   (Present perfect) _____

   _____

4. The teacher let me leave early.

   (Simple present) _____

   _____

5. The police officer instructed the driver to stay in the car.

   (Simple present) _____

   _____

6. He permits his patients to go home over the weekend.

   (Present perfect) _____

   _____

7. The proctor permitted the student to leave the room during the test.

   (Simple future) _____

   _____

8. I make him do his homework.

   (Present perfect) _____

   _____

9. The teacher does not let his students take a makeup test.

   (Simple past) _____

   _____

10. The teacher will never allow us to leave early.

    (Simple past) _____

    _____

INDEX

A

Ability, 151
Above, 70
Accident anecdotes, 141
Across from, 70
Action verbs, 18-19, 92
Active sentences, 201
Active voice, 200–201, 203
Adjective clauses, 118, 129–130
Adjectives, 116, 129
Adverb clauses, 231
   comparison, 232
   condition, 232
   contrast concession, 232
   manner, 232
   place, 232
   purpose, 232
   reason, 231
   result, 231
   time, 231
Advice, 151
A few, 48
Agreement, subject-verb, 21
A little, 48
Almost always, 43
A lot, 48
Also, 2445
Although, 232
Always, 43
Analysis of cause effect
   sentences, 145
Analyzing sentences that
   express a stance, 219
Anecdotes, 141
And, 180
Another, 72, 245
Argument, 229
Argumentation, 212
Argumentative paragraph, 211
   elements, 214
   supporting ideas, 224

Articles, 46
   a, 46
   an, 46
   the, 46
As, 231
As a result, 146, 180
As a result of, 146
At, 69
Attention grabber, 243
Auxiliary, 9
Awkward sentences, 13–14

B

Be brought about by, 146
Because, 146, 205
Be caused by, 146
Be due to, 146
Before, 70
Below, 70
Beneath, 70
Beside, 70
Between, 70
Be supposed to, 151, 153
Body paragraphs, 241, 244
Both...and, 181, 181
Brainstorming, 249
But, 180
By phrase, 207

C

Can, 151, 153, 155
Categories, 191
Categorizing ideas for an essay,
   249
Categorizing pierced parts by
   location, 67
Categorizing steps in a
   process, 65
Causal relationship, 137
Causative, 253
   allow, 256
   have, 253

   instruct, 256
   let, 253
   make, 253
   permit, 256
Cause and effect, 135
Cause and effect paragraph, 135
   concluding sentence, 139
   elements, 136
   support sentences, 137
   topic sentence, 136
Cause effect sentences, 147
Cause effect statements, 149
Characteristics, 77–78
Characters, 99
Chronological process, 55
Chronological order, 26, 61
Circular definition, 127
Class, 120
Classification, 185
Classification paragraph, 185
   concluding sentence, 192
   elements, 187
   topic sentence, 187
Classification sentences, 198
Classification sentences in active
   or passive, 192
Clauses, 10, 231
   dependent, 10, 231
   independent, 10, 231
Climax in narratives, 99
Coherence, 5
Colon, 200
Command, 108
Comma, 6
Comparison and contrast, 157
   concluding sentence, 165
   elements, 159
   support sentences, 162–164
   topic sentence, 160
Complement, 18
Complete sentence, 8–9
Complete thought, 9
Complex sentence, 234

Compound sentences, 176, 234
Concluding signal words and expressions, 57
Concluding paragraph, 248
Concluding sentence, 6, 32
    plan of action, 32
    prediction, 32
    recommendation, 32
    restatement, 32
Condition, adverb clauses, 232
Conjunction,
    coordination, 176
    subordination, 231
Conjunctive adverbs or adv. phrase, 180
Connectors, 244–245
    For first step in a process, 57
    second or subsequent step, 57
    final step, 57
Consequently, 146
Consistency, tense, 23
Contention, 227
Controlling idea, 3
Controversial issues, 227
Controversy, 227
Convincing supporting ideas, 25–26
Coordinating conjunctions, 176
Coordination, 176
Coordinators, 176
Correlative conjunctions, 181
Could, 153, 155
Could have, 155
Couldn't have, 155
Count nouns, 48
Criteria, 4, 8, 27

D

Debate, 227
Deciding what to compare and contrast, 169
Deciding whether to compare or contrast, 171
Definite article, 46
Definition sentence, 41, 113
Dependent clause, 8, 231
Describing a person, 82
Describing objects, 84

Describing scenery or view, 85
Description, 75
Descriptive paragraph, 75
    concluding sentence, 80
    elements, 77
    support sentences, 79
    topic sentence, 77
Despite the fact that, 232
Detailing support sentences, 30
Determination, 151
Determiners, 46
Determining class in extended definition, 120
Determining principles of classification, 195
Determining relevant ideas, 29
Differentiating between chronologically and spatially ordered paragraphs, 61
Directions, 41
Direct object, 14
Direct speech, 106
Disagreement, 229
Distinguishing characteristics, 122
Distinctive features, 99
Developing classification paragraph, 185

E

Editing, 22
Either...or, 181
Essay, 240
    attention grabber, 243
    body paragraphs, 244
    concluding paragraph, 248
    elements, 243
    thesis statement, 243
Essays, types of..., 245
Even though, 232
Example essay, 241
Example paragraph, 25–26
    concluding sentence, 32
    elements of, 27
    support sentences, 29
    topic sentence, 27
Expected behavior, 151
Expressing an opinion, 34

Extended definition, 111
    elements, 113
    single sentence definition as topic sentence, 113

F

Fables, 99, 101
Factual statement, 42–43
Fairy tales, 99, 101
Features, 77
Few, 48
Finally, 245
First, 245
Firstly, 245
First of all, 245
First person pronoun, 16
For, 146, 176
For example, 180
For instance, 180
Format, paragraph, 1
Fragments, 8–9
Frequency adverbs, 43–44
Furthermore, 180
Future tense, 9

G

Generating ideas, 2–3
Generating ideas for...
    argumentation, 227
    cause and effect, 140
    chronological paragraphs, 64
    classification, 196
    comparison and contrast, 166
    descriptive paragraphs, 81
    essays, 248
    extended definition, 120
    narratives, 104
    spatial paragraphs, 66
Giving reasons for your stance, 224

H

Habitual statement, 41
Had better, 151
Had to, 153, 153
Helping verb, 9
However, 164, 180

Hyphenated noun phrase, 114, 118

I

If, 232
In, 69
In addition, 180
Incomplete sentences, 8
In contrast, 162
Indentation, 1
Independent clause, 9, 10–11, 234
Indirect object, 14
In fact, 180
Infinitive, 253
Information about self, 41
Information question, 108
In front of, 70
In spite of, 232
Intransitive verb, 19–20
Introduction to the essay, 239
Issue, 189, 229

J

Just as, 163

L

Last but not least, 245
Like 163
Likewise, 163, 180
Linking verbs, 18
Listing distinguishing characteristics, 118
Listing similarities and differences, 173
Little, 48
Logical order of support sentences, 4–5
Lots, 48

M

Main idea of paragraph, 1
Many, 48
May, 151, 153
Might, 153, 153
Modal auxiliaries in cause effect sentences, 150

Modals, 151–155
    negative, 152
    other meanings, 151
    past, 153
    present, 151
Moral, 99
Moreover, 181
More than, 232
More… than, 232
Much, 48
Must, 151, 153, 155
Must have, 155

N

Narration, 99
Narrative paragraph, 99
    concluding sentence, 103
    elements, 101
    support, 102
    topic sentence, 101
Neither…nor, 181
Nevertheless, 181
Next to, 70, 215
Nimby, 198
Non-action verbs, 92
Non-count noun, 46–47
Non-idiomatic sentences, 13
Nor, 180
Not only…but also, 163, 181
Noun clauses, 94
Nouns, 15
    common, 15
    plural, 15
    proper, 15
    non-count, 15

O

Obligation, 151
Occasionally, 43
Often, 43
On, 69
On the left/right, 70
On the other hand, 162, 181
Opinion, 41
Or, 180
Ordering categories in classification, 191
Ordering steps in a process, 65

Ordinals 72
Other, 72
Others, 72
Over, 70

P

Paragraph analysis, 100
Paragraph format, 1
Paragraphs and essays: similarities and differences, 239
Participial adjectives, 208–209
Passive sentences, 201
Passive voice, 200–201, 203
Perfect tense, 9
Personal information, 45
Personal narrative, 99
Phrasal verbs, 71
Phrase, 8–9
Possibility, 151
Predicate, 14
Preference, 151
Prepositions, 69–72
    place, 69
    time, 69
Principles for classification, 196
Prioritizing ideas, 36
Process paragraph, 53
    concluding sentence, 59
    elements, 55
    topic sentence, 55
    support sentences, 57
Progressive tense, 8
Pronouns, 16
Proverbs, 104
Punctuating cause effect sentences, 147
Punctuating classification sentences, 200
Punctuation, 106, 200

Q

Quantifiers, 48
Quotation, 106

R

Reason, adverb clause, 232
Refutation, 225

Regret, 153
Relative pronoun, 94, 129
Relative clauses (*see* dependent clauses)
Relevance of support sentences in body paragraphs, 247
Relevant ideas, 29
Reported speech, 106
Restating a topic sentence, 192
Rough draft, 22

S

Sayings, 104
Second, 245
Secondly, 245
Second person pronoun, 16
Senses, 81
Sensory details, 87
Sentence types, 234
Setting, 99
Several, 48
Should, 151
Should have, 155
Signal words to end a paragraph, 6
Similarities, 180
Similarly, 180, 180
Similar to, 180
Simple present, 20, 40
Simple sentence, 180
    factual statements, 40
    habitual activities, 40
    opinion, 40
    personal information, 45
    use of…, 40–41
Since, 205
So, 147, 180
Some, 48
Sometimes, 43
Spatial process, 55
Spatial ordering, 67
Specific details, 30
Stance, 217–218
Statements, 94, 108
Stating the issue, 214

Story, 99
Subjects, 3, 15–17, 20
Subject/verb agreement, 105
Subject pronoun, 15
Subordination conjunction, 232
Subordinator, 150
Support sentences, 4

T

Taking a stand in argumentation, 217
    agree with, 217
    be against, 217
    be for, 217
    be in agreement with, 218
    be in support of, 218
    have qualms about, 218
    suppose, 217
    think, 217
That, 94, 129
The, 46
The most, 232
The other, 72
The others, 72
Thesis statement, 243
Third person pronoun, 16
Though, 232
Thus, 146
Time clauses, 231
    at the time of, 231
    co-occurrence, 231
    immediate, 231
    sequence, 231
To begin with, 244
Topic sentence, 3
Transition words and phrases,
Transitive verbs, 19–20
Types of sentences, 234

U

Unity, 4–5
Usually, 43
Unlike, 162

V

Verb, 8–9,
Verb phrase, 8–9, 43
Voice, 200–201
    active, 201
    passive, 201
Vocabulary in argumentation, 229

W

Warning, 151
Was supposed to, 153
Were supposed to, 153
What, 95
When, 95, 129
Where, 95, 129
Whereas, 162
Whether, 95
Which, 129
While, 162
Who, 129
Whom, 95, 129
Whose, 95, 129
Will, 151
Would, 155
Would have, 155
Would rather, 151
Would rather have, 153
Writing classification sentences, 198

Y

Yes/no question, 95, 108
Yet, 176
Yet another, 245
You, 15–16